# WHO SHALL LIVE?

# WHO SHALL LIVE?

the dilemma of
severely handicapped children
and its meaning for
other moral questions

## Leonard J. Weber

**PAULIST PRESS**
New York/Ramsey, N.J./Toronto

Library of Congress
Catalog Card Number: 76-18051

ISBN: 0-8091-1968-4

Published by Paulist Press
*Editorial Office:* 1865 Broadway, N.Y., N.Y. 10023
*Business Office:* 545 Island Road, Ramsey, N.J. 07446

Printed and bound in the
United States of America

# Contents

105245

*To*
*Frank and Mary,*
*my parents,*
*with love and gratitude*

# 1
# The Nature
# of the Question

As we live our everyday lives we sometimes get a glimpse of important decisions being made that may very well have an impact upon future practices (social and individual) and upon future attitudes and values. It is rarely easy to know the consequences of these decisions, but for anyone who is interested in the treatment of men by their fellowmen it is necessary to attempt to calculate the long-range consequences quickly and to take a stand while there may still be time to affect the outcome. The moral history of mankind is influenced by the ways in which the public responds to initial decisions made in certain areas.

It is not hard to find an example of decisions being made now by a few people that may seriously affect the future of all of us and of our children. In 1974 British gynecologist Dr. Douglas Bevis revealed that three babies had begun their lives in the laboratory. The ova, removed from women's ovaries, were kept alive in a bath of nutrients until fertilized by male sperm. The embryos were then inserted into the women's uteruses.[1] It is certainly not too soon to consider the social implications of this new technique of human reproduction and to contribute to the development of sound policies on laboratory fertilization and on human reproduction.

While the decisions being made at times to withhold treatment from severely handicapped infants may not strike some as having the same historical and dramatic impact as the decision to insert laboratory-fertilized ova into women's bodies, it is certainly one that needs to be given careful attention by all of us, not just by the few directly involved. In terms of the value that we attach to life itself, in terms of the implications of stressing that the quality of life is more important than the length of life, in terms of the treatment of the handicapped in our society, the response that is given to the decisions not to treat such infants is extremely important.

Some serious and well-considered reflections on the moral quality of the practice of not treating such infants have already been made. Much more needs to be done, however; both those who initially support and those who initially repudiate such decisions need to reflect deeply and publicly on the questions, so that the direction that we as a society take is a well-considered one. This work is one consideration of this major ethical dilemma.

As a way of initiating the study, this chapter focuses upon some examples of the decision to let an infant die, some reflections on reasons why this particular question has come to the forefront at this time, and an attempt to pinpoint the exact questions that need to be asked and answered in an ethical analysis of the practice.

*Some Cases*

In 1972, *Medical World News* provided its readers (mostly physicians) with some cases involving ethical problems. Since the purpose was to elicit the reader's response, the actual decisions in the cases on which the write-ups were based were not indicated. One of the cases involved an abnormal infant and clearly exemplifies the complexity of the decision that often needs to be made.

The baby was four days old and diagnosed as suffering from trisomy 18 [severe mental retardation in addition to physical malformation; most but not all of those affected die within the first year]. She was in a respirator. At a clinical conference, the chief of pediatrics reported on several agonizing conferences with the child's father, who had told him that if she would not be normal, "I don't want you to do anything for her." The chief had promised, "I will do everything in my power to see that your wishes are fulfilled."

The psychiatric consultant had also had several talks with the father. At the moment, he said, the father was in a stage of acute denial, but if the respirator were turned off at his initiative, later guilt feelings could cause psychiatric problems. On the other hand, there could also be guilt feelings if the family took the child home, only to have her die later. The psychiatric social worker characterized the father differently and said she thought the family would be put under extreme stress if the child were brought home.

The nurse who had been caring for the infant was burning with outrage. The baby could not be allowed to die. If necessary, she herself would try to adopt the child and take care of her.

A pediatrics resident called attention to the case of another baby who had a respiratory difficulty; he thought this child should be put on a respirator and without it ran a 50-50 chance of brain damage. But all the other respirators in the hospital were being used by patients who had critically pressing need for them.[2]

One of the questions raised by this case is the question of who should be the one to make the decision of whether this child should be treated any further (for some unknown reason, the mother is not mentioned in this case study). Other questions revolve around the concept of "quality of life." Does it imply physiological and psychological normalcy and should a more normal child be treated at the expense of a less normal one? Should the decision be affected by the concern for the psychological well-being of the family?

In its September 1973 issue, *The Hastings Center Report* presented the following case:

Missy, the daughter of Mike and Sue B., was born with spina bifida with meningomyelocele, a defect which occurs approximately once in every 500 live births. Spina bifida refers to an abnormal opening in the spine, and meningomyelocele is a condition in which portions of the spinal cord, as well as meninges and spinal fluid, have slipped out through the abnormal opening and are enclosed in a sac which protrudes from the backbone. Up until ten years ago, almost 80% of these babies were certain to die in early infancy. Today, surgical treatment is available to ameliorate the condition, and about 75% now survive, although affected children all face a lifetime of illness, operations and varying degrees of disability, including mental retardation.

. . . Without surgery, he (the physician) said, Missy would probably contract meningitis which, if untreated, would either lead to more severe handicaps or even be fatal. He explained further that if Missy survived an operation, she would never be able to walk without the aid of braces and crutches, that she would have to undergo extensive physical therapy all her life, and that she had a 90% chance of developing hydrocephalus ("water on the brain").

Sue and Mike decided not to have Missy treated.[3]

The parents later changed their minds and decided to have Missy treated, but the ethical nature of their first decision, accepted by the staff, can be considered in itself. Does the fact that with treatment the chances are very good that Missy would survive impose any sort of a moral obligation to treat? It is often argued, in the cases of adult dying patients, that there may come a time when treatment only prolongs the dying and suffering, so that it would be better to "let die." But in the case of someone like Missy, where no treatment leads to deterioration and not immediately to death, what constitutes "letting die" and what constitutes neglect or refusal to provide ordinary care?

Another example of the decision not to treat was presented

in *The Atlantic Monthly*, April 1968. A father spoke of his mongoloid son. The following excerpts from the longer account reflect, I think, the spirit of the father's decision and attitude:

> There was no doubt at all about the diagnosis, said Dr. L. No tests were necessary. All the classic symptoms were present. The child, he said, would be vulnerable to heart trouble "of a severe sort," perhaps at age one or two. He would be peculiarly susceptible to digestive ailments and respiratory troubles. Life would, according to medical experience, be short. Mental development would be arrested at the age level of two or three.

> Dr. L. said many parents institutionalize mongolian children, "particularly when there is another child at home, a normal child . . ."

> I told Dr. K. that I wanted nothing done to extend my son's hold on life artificially. He assured me he understood. The sanitarium, he said, contains no oxygen. The children are given no inoculations against childhood diseases, unless parents insist. "There are churches on all sides of me," he said. "Everyone of these ministers agrees with me that it would not be moral, or serving God's will, to prolong these lives."

> At the suggestion of an official in the welfare department, a social caseworker took Philip to the sanitarium next day. I had brought her diapers, nightgowns, blankets, bunting, and bottles for his formula. A few hours after Philip's arrival, Dr. K. called to tell me he had died. "Heart failure and jaundice," he said. "Consider it a blessing. . . ."

> I did not know my son. I do not know his thousands of brothers and sisters, of whom it has been written, "Oh, what a mortal pity he was ever born," and I do not know the parents of these children. I do not speak for them, just for myself and perhaps for Philip. I believe that it is time for a

sane and civilized and humane approach to euthanasia.

I don't know how it should be practiced, or what committee
should have a voice in the decisions, or what pill or injection
might best be employed. I do know that there are thousands
of children on this earth who should never have been born.
Their lives are a blank. They do not play; they do not read;
they do not grow; they do not live nor love. Their life is
without meaning to themselves, and an agony to their families.[4]

As is indicated above, the practice of doing very little to extend the lives of deformed children has long existed in institutions. The children are kept clean and clothed and fed, and
medical emergencies like bleeding and choking are taken care
of, but they are not even protected against childhood diseases.
Is this different from not treating a particular disease? Are the
lives of the deformed, as the author argued, really without
meaning? If the life is not considered worth living, would it not ·
be appropriate to take active steps to end that life?

The most famous and widely discussed case of not treating
a baby with Down's syndrome (mongolism) has been re-enacted
in the film "Who Should Survive?" by the Joseph P. Kennedy,
Jr. Foundation, 1972. The incident took place at Johns Hopkins
Hospital and involved the decision on the part of parents not to
permit an operation that was necessary so that the child could
be fed normally. The baby, in addition to its mongolism, was
suffering from duodenal atresia, bowel obstruction. Unless an
operation were performed to correct this condition, the baby
could not be fed by mouth. The operation is not a major one in
itself, but in a small baby must be considered fairly serious. The
parents refused to permit the operation, choosing to let the baby
die from lack of food. It was fifteen days until the baby finally
died.

The case, as it is presented in the film, makes one point
perfectly evident. The operation was refused not in any way
because of the unusual nature of that procedure itself; if such an
operation had been necessary for an otherwise normal baby,

there is every indication that the parents would have immediately consented and that the staff would have defended the right of the child to treatment (by way of court if necessary). The decision not to treat was clearly based on the fact that the child had Down's syndrome and could expect the abnormal and arrested development of such children.

In March, 1974, the following item appeared in the press. It represents the response of one justice to the decision not to treat and the practice of treating unequal children (unequal in terms of their capability for normal life) unequally.

Portland, Me.—David Patrick Houle was born February 9 in the Maine Medical Center here with much of his left side malformed.

There was no left eye. The left ear had no ear canal. A left thumb was malformed. Some of his vertebrae were not fused. There was an opening between his windpipe and his esophagus. He could be fed only intravenously.

If he survived, doctors said, he would be partly deaf, palsied, blind and mentally retarded.

The baby's parents . . . decided not to permit life-prolonging surgery. The medical center took the matter to a state court, and the court made medical history—by ordering the hospital to perform the necessary surgery.

. . . Justice David G. Roberts ruled that the "issue before the court is not the prospective quality of the life to be preserved . . . At the moment of live birth there does exist a human being entitled to the fullest protection of the law. The most basic right is the right to life itself."

Acknowledging the adverse impact his ruling might have on the parents, the judge said the issue was "the almost certain risk of death should treatment be withheld."[5]

It is difficult to calculate the full impact of Justice Roberts' ruling. Clearly one of the questions it raises is the question of whether everything must always be attempted to prolong the lives of children, regardless of the future prospects in terms of survival and in terms of quality of life. Is that approach the only alternative to a policy of letting parents decide totally for themselves which children should live and which should not?

In an article in *The New England Journal of Medicine*, Raymond Duff and A. G. Campbell of the Yale-New Haven Hospital special care nursery revealed that 43 out of 299 deaths were associated with discontinuance or withdrawal of treatment.

Some examples of management choices . . . illustrate the problems. An infant with Down's syndrome and intestinal atresia, like the much-publicized one at Johns Hopkins Hospital, was not treated because his parents thought that surgery was wrong for their baby and themselves. He died seven days after birth. Another child had chronic pulmonary disease . . . by five months of age, he still required 40% oxygen to survive, and even then, he was chronically dyspneic and cyanotic [breathed with difficulty and showed blueness of skin, as from imperfectly oxygenated blood]. The nurses, parents and physicians considered it cruel to continue, and yet difficult to stop. All were attached to this child, whose life they had tried so hard to make worthwhile. The family had endured high expenses (the hospital bill exceeding $15,000), and the strains of the illness were believed to be threatening the marriage bonds and to be causing sibling behavioral disturbances. Oxygen supplementation was stopped, and the child died in about three hours. . . .

Arguments among staff members and families for and against such decisions were based on varied notions of the rights and interests of defective infants, their families, professionals, and society. . . . Regarding the infants, some contended that individuals should have a right to die in some circumstances such as anencephaly, hydranencephaly, and some severely deforming and incapacitating conditions. Such very defective individuals were considered to have little or no hope of achieving meaningful "humanhood." For example, they have little or no capacity to love or be loved. . . .

When maximum treatment was viewed as unacceptable by families and physicians in our unit, there was a growing tendency to seek early death as a management option, to avoid that cruel choice of gradual, often slow, but progressive deterioration of the child who was required under these circumstances in effect to kill himself. Parents and the staff then asked if his dying needed to be prolonged. If not, what were the most appropriate medical responses?[6]

Many other examples could be presented, but the above (all taken from publicly available sources) are sufficient to describe the nature of the practice of not treating severely handicapped infants and to initiate reflection on the nature of the ethical problem facing the public. It is not a new problem that we are dealing with, but one that is forcing itself upon us with special intensity at the present time.

## *Why Now?*

A major reason for the present intensity of the question of whether we should treat the severely handicapped infant is that we are having very serious reservations about some of the accomplishments of modern medicine. Most Americans probably know some relative, neighbor, or friend who, if it had not been for the tremendous advances of medical science in the last century, would have died long ago but who now is living a normal or nearly normal life. These experiences account for our overall high approbation of the medical profession. Many Americans, however, also know about individuals whose lives have been extended by modern medical science but at a cost that may have been very high. They have not been cured or healed; perhaps they simply lived longer in pain and suffering. They have not been cured or healed; perhaps their symptoms have been relieved but they live to have children and pass on their genetic disease. They have not been cured or healed; perhaps they live from infancy on as a burden on their families.

There appears to be a growing conviction that not all the possible accomplishments of modern medicine are to be pursued, even if it means that life is somewhat shortened. This conviction is sometimes expressed in different ways or focused on different dimensions of the problem. Only a couple of the forms this thinking takes can be looked at here.

One common expression of the conviction that not all possible procedures should be undertaken to prolong life is the emphasis on quality of life as opposed to quantity of life. There is a fully developed quality of life ethic that will need to be considered later; what is of concern here is the widespread expression of the need to emphasize the type of life that is being prolonged. As the concept is being used here, "quality of life" merely indicates that it is possible to do more harm than good in medicine, that there are times when it is better not to extend life if there is much suffering as a result. To advocate concern for the quality of life is a way of emphasizing the necessity to minimize undesired consequences. In the cases of abnormal infants, this concern for the consequences of prolonging life highlights the possible effects such actions would have upon the child, the family, and society.

First of all, the consequences for the child himself need to be considered. The handicapped infant can expect a life of physical suffering and/or of inability to achieve full mental potential. Can this suffering be prevented in a way that in itself does not increase suffering or produce other undesirable consequences?

Second, what are the probable consequences for the parents and family of the handicapped? The personal anguish and suffering that they will have to endure in caring for the unusual child might be very great. There is also the economic and social cost to the family of having such a child.

Third, there is the question of the possible suffering of society. Taxpayers may have to assume some of the costs involved in caring for these children. And others may suffer as a result of the use of scarce resources to maintain the lives of handicapped children. The decision should take into account the fact that these, too, may be some of the undesired consequences.

The emphasis on the quality of life and on the possible unpleasant consequences of extending life is one manner of expressing the concern that medical science not become cold and calculate only quantity. Science must have a heart, and a heart is motivated by the hope of decreasing suffering.

Another explanation for the fact that the question of whether to treat handicapped infants is so important today may be the recently awakened realization that the survival of some of us now may be detrimental to future generations. In a sense, this is a further extension of the previously discussed concern for suffering. This genetic awareness focuses on our obligation as regards the health of future generations, our obligation not to impose suffering upon them by our decisions now.

Modern medicine has enabled many people who are carriers of genetic defects and who would have died before the age of reproduction in the past to live to produce children and pass on the defect. "For this reason scientists speak of the increasing pollution or degeneration of the genetic pool."[7] The number of people with genes for defects is increasing as a direct result of medicine's success in keeping genetically diseased persons alive. "What benefits the living individual and the present generation is bad for the human race as a whole and bad for future generations."[8]

Diabetes can be used as an example. Diabetics formerly died early. After successful treatment was found in insulin, diabetics could survive and live useful lives, though most were still not able to have children. Now, of course, the children of diabetic mothers can be delivered safely. The result of these two steps in medical progress is that the incidence of diabetes in the population is increasing. "Of course we can get along with a lot more diabetics, and with good medical care they can live happily and bear diabetic children of their own. But there is a limit beyond which this process cannot be carried, and if we consider not diabetes alone, but all other ills to which the human race is genetically heir, that limit is not far away."[9]

The realization that the genetic pool is degenerating has probably been a great influence in bringing the question of handicapped infants to the forefront at this time. It provides some scientific support for the contention that prolonging lives now often leads to more suffering later and that this later suffering may greatly outweigh the individual benefit. The discovery that "though it was long before we realized it, conventional medicine emerged as one of the greatest threats to the human race"[10] gives great power to the claim that we must think twice before applying all possible medical techniques.

In addition, the focus on the genetically affected naturally leads us to focus on the health of the young, the infant, and the fetus. The quality of the genetic pool is not going to be affected by prolonging the life of someone past child-producing age. But it may very well be affected by prolonging the life of someone who is not yet of child-producing age. And though not every congenital disease or abnormality (one present at birth) means that the parents are carriers or that it can be passed on genetically, there is, naturally enough, a tendency to relate all birth defects to genetic health. Thus, the realization that the genetic health of the race is often adversely affected by medical interventions translates into a question about saving the life of this abnormal child.

The desire to relieve or prevent suffering and the concern for how medicine affects the genetic health of the race are two important reasons why there is at present a great deal of doubt about the wisdom of medical intervention in the case of severely handicapped infants. These are not the only contemporary discussions and movements that have contributed to the question; two more can be indicated. One is the question of what constitutes human life. The other is the general movement toward an acceptance of death.

There are two different ways in which phrases like "full human life" or "meaningful humanhood" have become part of our contemporary conversation. One is the maximal sense, what constitutes real humanness of the type that we ought to aspire to, what is the ideal, the goal. In this sense what is really human is equated with the achievement of our full potential as men and women. The question about humanness is also being asked on the minimal level. Here the concern is for what constitutes the minimum that "someone" must be or have or do before we should accept him as one of us, as possessor of all the basic rights that one has by the very fact that he is a member of the race. While both senses of "humanness" are of importance to those who are dealing with severely handicapped infants, it is the second sense, the minimal sense, that is of more importance.

The primary example of the question of minimal humanness in recent years has been the question of when human life begins. Is a fetus really human? Is it homicide, the killing of a human, to kill a fetus? Is a two-week-old embryo human? A nine-week fetus? Human at age of viability? These are the very common questions that anyone familiar with the abortion discussion has seen again and again. They remain very important questions. A large segment of the population and the majority of Supreme Court justices have decided that a pre-viable fetus is not fully human or that, at least for practical purposes, we can act as though it is not human. Another large segment of the society insists that the fetus has as much right to life as you or I and is just as human.

What the question of minimal humanness asks is precisely whether animal life of the species *homo sapiens* is sufficient reason to designate someone human or whether more than physical life is necessary. And once this question has been asked, as it has over and over in the abortion question, then it becomes possible to ask the same question of those members of the species who have long ago or just recently emerged from their mothers' bodies. One may very well want to answer the question differently for those within the womb and for those outside, but the question of whether the life of the human body is enough to constitute humanhood can and will be asked of both.

In addition to the abortion controversy, the question of what constitutes humanhood has been asked in the discussion of when death occurs. The problem of a clinical definition of death is another question that has been raised by the success of modern medicine. Mechanical equipment like respirators can keep a person breathing and his heart beating long after the body is able to carry on these functions on its own. Is such a person alive? The question of the time of death is sometimes related to a transplant operation. If the organ is to be used after death, it will be kept in best condition if the blood is kept circulating. Is it possible, then, to believe someone dead if his heart is still beating? What constitutes human life and when has human life ended?

For the most part, the practical solution to the problem has been to recognize that it is possible for someone to be dead even though his heart and lungs continue to function with the help of mechanical equipment. At the same time these traditional signs of life are important in the determination of death in that one of the tests used is the turning off of the equipment to see if there is any spontaneous attempt to breathe. If there is, the person is not yet declared dead, no matter how "dead" his brain appears to be. Thus, the so-called "brain-death" approach is not, strictly speaking, that. It does acknowledge, though, that a person may be dead even when some of his bodily functions continue only because of machines.[11]

There are some who are proposing a true brain-death definition of death, one that would permit physicians to declare a person dead even when (theoretically and probably in some rare cases) that person's heart and lungs may function without the help of a machine. The argument is made that human death should be recognized as neocortical death, for "the death of the neocortex marks the end of the physiological basis for human consciousness, that is, a consciousness unique in its powers of reflection."[12] Though there may be enough life in the brain stem to keep bodily functions going, what is alive is no longer a human person. "With the death of the neocortex, the potentiality to reflect consciously is eradicated in the organism."[13] And it is the ability to reflect consciously that makes a person a person.

The attempt to find a satisfactory solution to the problem of when to declare someone dead has raised the question of whether human life is to be equated with physical life of the human species, the very same question raised by the attempt to find a satisfactory solution to the question of abortion. These attempts to determine just what it means to be really human constitute an atmosphere where the true humanness of the severely retarded infant is questioned. Some have suggested that a child with Down's syndrome is not human. "To be a human is to be self-aware, consciously related to others, capable of rationality in a measure at least sufficient to support some initiative . . . a Down's is not a person."[14] While there is much disagreement with that position, there can be no doubt that the whole discussion of what constitutes human life is one of the reasons why the question of what to do with deformed infants is so important today.

One more factor can be mentioned as contributing to the contemporary importance of the deformed infant problem. This is society's new-found awareness of death. Among certain segments of Americans, at least, it is becoming increasingly common to talk about death. Many books and articles have been written about death, death is a popular topic on the public lecture circuit, and courses on death and dying have been introduced in many colleges and high schools. It is very difficult at the present time to assess the overall significance of this new death awareness, but there can be no doubt that it is a reality.

One of the forms this new awareness of death is taking is the attempt to understand the attitude of dying patients themselves toward their own death. The most well-known work in this area is that of Dr. Kubler-Ross.[15] Through her work with dying patients, she came to recognize that most dying persons go through various stages from denial and anger to an eventual acceptance of their own impending deaths. Two of her findings seem to make a special impact upon the many readers of her studies. The first is her observation that most persons, given the time and opportunity, will come to terms with the fact of death and die in relative peace. Death, when it finally comes, is often not fought against. In addition, Kubler-Ross' interviews with dying patients revealed to her the need these people have to talk about their own deaths and to have help in working through their own feelings. Many times they know they are dying long before they are told and they know it even in the face of attempts on the part of physician and family to pretend otherwise. Her interviews with dying patients have taught that it is frequently not doing the patient a service to refuse to talk with him or her about death.

Another way in which the new death awareness is manifested is in what might be called the "death is natural" school of thought. This encompasses many people with varying viewpoints—from the back-to-nature enthusiasts to champions of consumers' rights. They all, however, have at least one point in common—they are opposed to the extent to which contemporary society goes to, in a sense, pretend that death is not a fact of life. The "death is natural" movement criticizes contemporary American funeral practices. The act of preparing someone to be viewed by friends and relatives is seen as an attempt to hide the fact of death, to make it less likely that we will be forced to come to terms with our own mortality. They see extravagant coffins and funerals not so much as a way of honoring the dead as a money-grabbing racket. In general, common ways of dealing with death are viewed as involving sham and the exploitation of the family; the way to begin to correct some of these cultural deficiencies is through the realization that death is natural.

A third manifestation of the new awareness of death is the "death with dignity" movement. This movement takes many forms and not all those who are being grouped together here like the "death with dignity" banner or agree with others who are being placed with them. The term is simply used here to describe a common desire to make it possible that death be as meaningful and human as possible. For some this means the public recognition that not every means needs to be employed to prolong life when there is no hope for recovery, that we can do better than to have the patient die alone with the family having been replaced by tubes and machines and the harried hospital staff. To others "death with dignity" will be provided for much better once the states have legalized mercy killing. When this is done, it will be possible to choose the time to administer as easy a death as possible, with as much suffering as possible avoided. Another attempt to provide for a better way of caring for the dying is the whole notion of a hospice, on the order of St. Christopher's Hospital in England. Here the whole purpose is to care for the dying as they are dying, and not in any way to pretend that they are being cured. Staff members spend much of their time visiting with the patients and family members are always welcome. The hospice is wholly dedicated to caring for terminal patients, with the personnel fully trained to make the lives of the dying as interesting and fulfilled as possible.

These various dimensions of the new awareness of death include a number of very different perspectives, but they all combine to increase acceptance of death. More and more, the idea appears to be growing that there really is "a time to die." It is easy to see how this growing acceptance of death is one of the factors contributing to the importance of the question of severely handicapped infants. If death is not always unwelcome, then perhaps it is not totally inappropriate to consider death as an option in the treatment of these children.

## The Ethical Issues

This book is devoted to the question, in all its complexities, of the morality of the decision not to treat severely handicapped infants. The question is not one simple question. To clarify the issues involved and the questions that need to be answered in any study of this sort, we can divide the question into three separate considerations.

First, should the principle be accepted that it may be ethical at times *not* to treat? Is there any moral justification for the practice of making no attempt to save the life of an infant, someone who has no capacity yet of declaring his own desire for life or for death? Is it in any way a violation of sound medical and ethical procedures for parents and medical personnel to decide that no attempt shall be made to preserve the life of some child? Or is the only morally defensible position one that insists that everything must always be done to keep an infant alive, no matter what his condition? If it is proper not to treat at times, what exactly is the moral justification? What is the good that is being served by such actions? What are the consequences and the long-range implications of adopting such a principle?

If the first question is answered in the negative (that there is no moral justification for ever declining treatment), then there are no further questions. If the first question is answered in the affirmative (that there may be times when the decision to let die rather than treat is morally justified), then other questions follow.

If the decision not to treat is morally justified at times, what are those times? Which infants should not be treated? Does the decision depend upon the nature of the abnormality and on the prognosis for physical and mental health with treatment? If so, how bad should the condition be before withholding treatment is justified? Do prospects for a reasonably normal life with treatment impose a moral obligation to treat? Or does the justification for the decision not to treat depend also upon factors other than the health of the child, such as the ability of the parents to cope emotionally and financially with the care of a handicapped child? Should the decision be left entirely up to the parents? Or should there be limits to parental discretion in this regard? What might the limits be? How can guidelines be established to help make the decision-making process easier and to guard against abuses?

All the ethical questions are not yet answered when the decision to treat or not to treat a particular child is made. Does the decision to treat initially mean that there can be no justification for reversing that decision later? What should be done with those who are not treated? Would it be more humanitarian to induce death directly if they would not die immediately otherwise? Would it be better for the parents to keep their distance from the child so as not to suffer so much at the loss?

These are the questions that must be answered for a full moral understanding of the handicapped infant issue. Some of the questions may be found only in those cases. Some are raised as well by other issues, especially those like abortion and euthanasia, which also concern the moral legitimacy of letting die and killing. Certainly our discussion cannot proceed in a vacuum; it must be aware of the context provided by the on-going debate on those topics.

# 2
# The Ethical Context

When parents are faced with a decision regarding a helpless infant, seriously ill and dependent for future life upon the decisions those parents make, the situation cannot but be emotion-laden and agonizing. It is not necessary to point to any larger context to indicate the significance of the kind of decision that is made.

Nevertheless, one of the reasons why the question of whether or not to treat deformed infants (or which ones to treat) has emerged as one of the most significant questions in medical ethics is that it *is* part of a larger context. A debate has long centered on the question of the value of life in regard to abortion and euthanasia and that debate shows no signs of ending soon. Whether one wants it to be or not, our question regarding deformed infants is going to be seen in the context of this debate on the value of life. Indeed, the ethical ramifications of a moral stance taken on this question can only be understood by examining the abortion-euthanasia context.

This chapter may not make the task of answering the questions raised in the first chapter any easier. But it will, hopefully, provide some of the background necessary to make those answers wise ones.

## Abortion

The heated debate on the morality of abortion in recent years has made everyone aware of the fact that there are widespread differences of opinion in our society on the acceptability of the procedure. Though all are aware of the debate, the real significance of the issues is not always made clear in the heat of the fight. It is necessary to look briefly again at the debate and analyze carefully the different positions that are being taken.

Looking only at the moral positions and not at the stands taken on legal policy, it is useful to distinguish four different approaches. It is not, I think, doing an injustice to any of the many positions on the morality of abortion to place them all in one of these four general positions:

1. Direct abortion is never morally acceptable.
2. Direct abortion is morally acceptable only if necessary to save the life of the mother.
3. Abortion is morally acceptable for a certain number of ascertainable reasons, but not for all reasons or on request.
4. Abortion is morally acceptable whenever the woman wants it.

The first position begins with a consideration of what an abortion involves. It is the direct destruction of human life, innocent human life. The life of the human fetus should be treated, at least for all practical purposes, as full human life; there is not sufficient reason to consider it anything other than human and the benefit of any doubt there may be should be given to the protection of life. A human person may be legitimately killed only when, by his own actions, he has forfeited his right to life. Thus, for example, it is morally acceptable to kill someone when acting against unjust aggression, as in an act of self-defense or while participating in a just war. The human fetus is incapable of any action which would constitute unjust aggression. He is innocent and, therefore, his life may never be legitimately taken directly.

This is a very strong anti-abortion stand. Its point is that everything else follows from respect for life itself. Concern about the quality of the life of the mother and of the life of the baby is admirable, but there is a great danger of destroying that quality in the pursuit of it if a certain basic respect is not given to the inviolability of life itself. You must have life before you can have a good life. Those who take this stand are not unsympathetic toward the plight of the mother; they cannot condone, however, the violence of killing as a solution to the problem.

This position has been described as being opposed to all "direct" abortion because most proponents of this view, including the Roman Catholic Church, accept "indirect" abortion when done for proportionate reasons. By indirect abortion is meant "any instance in which a treatment or operative procedure is performed for some other purpose but incidentally and secondarily does cause the expulsion of the fetus."[1] This is seen as morally acceptable only when there is a very serious risk to the woman's life in not having the procedure done immediately. An example would be of a woman whose cancerous uterus must be removed to preserve her life. This is acceptable even if it means the fetus will die. The difference between a direct abortion and an indirect abortion is that a direct abortion is the attempt to accomplish a desirable purpose by an evil act of killing while an indirect abortion involves an evil element only as an unfortunate secondary effect. It is necessary to be concerned about the consequences of one's actions, of course, but all unfortunate consequences cannot always be avoided and, for proportionate reasons, they can be permitted.

The second position is very similar to the first; as far as most cases of abortion go, it is an unacceptable solution to problems. This is also generally recognized as an anti-abortion position that puts the emphasis on the necessity to respect and protect the life of the human fetus. It does, however, differ in one significant way from the previous stand. It finds abortion acceptable when the mother's life can be saved in no other way. In analyzing the reasons that justify killing, it puts less emphasis on the innocence or guilt of the one who is the aggressor and more emphasis on the fact that a life is being directly threatened. To save her own life a woman is morally justified in having an abortion as a type of self-defense. This position insists, though, that nothing less than life itself is sufficient justification for killing the fetus. Our social life will become intolerable if we begin to take lives for any lesser reason.

The third position includes a variety of individual positions, but they all have one belief in common: there are more reasons which justify the killing of a fetus than justify the killing of someone after birth. They also all agree that the fetus must be seen as having some claims to our respect and protection so it would not be acceptable to have an abortion except for a serious reason.

The reasons given as serious enough to warrant an abortion vary from individual to individual within this group. The usual reasons include these: if the physical or emotional health of the woman would be seriously harmed by pregnancy or the rearing of a child; if the pregnancy is the result of rape or incest; if there is serious reason to think that the child will be born with a grave physical or mental defect; if some other serious personal or social complication exists (such as the extreme youth of the pregnant girl or a severe problem of overpopulation). Fetal life is good and is to be protected generally, but there are also other values that have to be protected. Sometimes abortion is an acceptable way of protecting these goods.

Not all who approve of abortion in some cases but not in others are in agreement on whether fetal life should be considered human. Most concede some element of humanness but not yet the full personal life that is present in those who are more fully developed. Thus it is justifiable to kill a fetus with less reason that it would take to kill a child after birth (and thus, for some, the greater reason needed the longer pregnancy continues). It is not the same to intervene to prevent the development of a life to full humanhood at this early stage as it is to end the life of someone, no longer in the womb, who is clearly among us as one of us. The concern that the new life not be destroyed has to be balanced against concern for the quality of life of others and the quality of life of that potential baby himself. Is it not better for the woman, her family, and society if she protects her health even if it means an abortion? The value gained is greater than what is lost. It is better for the woman who is pregnant as a result of rape to have an abortion than to suffer the constant reminder of that terrible aggression. In all the cases where abortion is justified by this position, it is done on the basis of this sort of balancing of what is gained against what is lost. The fetus' life counts for something, perhaps much, but not so much that it is proper that the woman, the family, or society should suffer seriously as a result of not taking the opportunity to end that life.

This third position is generally considered a pro-abortion stand, and it is. It has very serious disagreements with the abortion-on-request morality, however. It insists that fetal life is to be considered an important value and no reasons of mere convenience or of mild hardship are justification for ending that life. Some reasons, those that are very serious, justify abortion, but not just any reason. Abortion is not to be adopted simply as an easy way out or as a matter of total moral inconsequence.

The final position is the abortion-on-request position. Abortion here is seen as morally acceptable whenever it is freely chosen by the woman, for whatever reason. Abortion is immoral only when a woman is forced to have an abortion when she does not want one.

The primary good that needs to be protected in the ethics of the maternal-fetal relationship is the right of the woman to control her own reproductive behavior. It is her own body that is involved and it is essential that she be free to do whatever she thinks best with that body and its reproductive processes. And this moral value of freedom can only be defended by recognizing that any reason that seems sufficient to the woman herself is moral justification for ending fetal life. The real issue is not whether the fetus has a right to life but whether we want to impose mandatory motherhood by insisting that there are some reasons for which the woman is not morally justified in removing the fetus from her body.

The value of the fetus' life is described in different ways by different spokespersons for this position. For some, the fetus is seen as part of the woman's body or as a form of animal life but clearly not as independent human life. It is not capable of any of the activities that we normally associate with a human being. For others, the question of whether a fetus is a human person is simply the wrong question to ask. That is a question of biological fact and the decision to abort or not to abort has to be made on other grounds, on the basis of values. The health and welfare and autonomy of the woman are primary considerations. The family situation and the probable life for the child are also very important. These are matters of conscience for the woman involved and cannot be decided by an answer to the question of when the fetus should be considered human.

In addition to the emphasis on the moral value of the woman's freedom, the abortion-on-request position also makes a major point of whether a baby is wanted or not. It is wrong to bring an unwanted child into the world. The influences upon a child's life are so important in determining whether that life will be a fullfilled and happy one, and the child who is unwanted is starting against tremendous odds. If we are at all concerned about the quality of life, we will agree that no unwanted child should ever be born. The fact that the woman does not want a baby at this time can make abortion a responsible and moral act.

As this brief review of the four major positions on the morality of abortion indicates, the chief issue is very clearly the value of fetal life. The question of how valuable (good, important, protectable, sacred) the life of the human fetus is has been answered differently by the different stands on abortion (though the difference between the first and the second positions in this regard is negligible).

Sometimes the abortion discussion focuses on the question of when human life begins. As Daniel Callahan has analyzed the question in his classic study on abortion,[2] there are basically three schools of opinion. The genetic school argues that human life begins at conception, when the genetic code is fixed. From this moment the individual is whoever he will become; he only grows and develops thereafter. The developmental school holds that at least some development is necessary before this life is a human person in any meaningful sense. Within the developmental school of thought there is some disagreement on precisely when the conceptus becomes human; some use a criterion of brain development, others see organ development as decisive, others consider viability the determining factor. The third school is the social consequences school. This school rejects all biological factors as important. We (adult human beings) decide what human life is and such decisions need to take into account the kind of social policy people want. If, in our abortion policy, we do not choose to treat the fetus as human, then it is not. What constitutes human life is a matter of social policy, not a fact.

When human life begins and what constitutes that beginning are important issues, but the issue can more clearly be understood as one of value—how valuable is fetal life and to what can we compare that value. The abortion positions are sometimes based on objective attempts to determine what evidence about the beginning of human life is most compelling. More often, however, the positions are arrived at after wrestling with the questions of how important that life is and what the effects would be upon those immediately involved now and upon our social life in the long run if that life were to be destroyed. We want to know what that life counts for, especially as compared to other values.

The four abortion positions have three different answers (the first and second positions can be joined) to the question of what fetal life counts for. The first says that it counts for as much as your life or mine; just as there can be no peace in the world and no hope for quality of life without considering your life and mine inviolable, so in the long run all of us may suffer seriously if we do not protect the life of the fetus. A society is most healthy, morally and socially, when it protects the weak and the helpless against aggression. Abortion destroys the weak and helpless in the name of the quality of life of the stronger. If we do not let the fetus count for as much as we do, we are establishing a policy of inequality and discrimination at the very time when we are priding ourselves for beginning to rise above racial and religious and sexual discrimination. To count the fetus as less than ourselves is to justify the gravest form of discrimination (extermination) based upon stage or condition of life, something we ordinarily consider repugnant.

The third abortion position argues that the fetus' life counts for something less than what yours and mine count for. The fetus' life has to count for something and it has to count for something very important, otherwise we fail to recognize that

whatever is of some human quality has value. If we do not respect the life of the fetus, we are devaluing human life somewhat
and respect for the value of human life is the necessary heart of
our social morality. But respect for fetal life does not mean
absolute respect; its life does not count for that much. To say
that there is no more justification for killing a fetus than for
killing you or me is to turn a deaf ear to the real needs of pregnant women. It may be an indication of the ambiguity and tragedy of human life, but there are situations where the preservation of the life of the fetus means ignoring real needs of the
woman or her family. The same thing is true on a larger scale.
If society turns its primary attention to protecting the lives of
fetuses, it would be saying that mere survival is more important
than the quality of the lives of those people already born. Is
there not a danger that we may ignore the problems of poverty,
hunger, and injustice (quality of life concerns) if we say that the
survival of the fetus is more important than the quality of life of
the woman? For our social and moral health, therefore, we cannot let the fetus count for too much.

The final abortion position argues that, for all practical
purposes, the life of the fetus counts for nothing. The fetus may
have some value, but it cannot be considered to count for so
much that a woman would ever consider killing it a moral evil.
To consider the life of the fetus to be worth that much is already to have values out of focus. One of the most basic values
in any healthy individual and any healthy society is the freedom
of the individual to act as he or she wishes in the private sphere
of life. Just as we need to be concerned about poverty and
hunger and injustice in our society and in the world, so we need
to be concerned about unfreedom. To say that the fetus' life is
of such a value that it should not be taken or can only be taken
for certain reasons is to unjustifiably reduce a woman's freedom.

Thus the issue is focused squarely on the value of undeveloped life. And, as will be seen, the question of whether to
treat severely deformed infants encounters a similar concern at
times, a concern for the value of the life of someone very different from most of us. The abortion debate, at least in that
sense, is not separate from our concern.

One particular type of abortion situation is even more closely related to the deformed infant dilemma. That is "selective abortion," abortion undertaken solely because it is known or there is reason to suspect that the baby will not be normal. In cases of selective abortion, it is not a pregnancy that is unwanted; it is not a baby that is unwanted; it is, rather, a particular unhealthy child that is unwanted. If the fetus were normal, no abortion would be performed.

Pre-natal testing has been becoming increasingly common as scientists have learned to diagnose many defects before birth. Amniocentesis is the most successful method of pre-natal testing. It involves the withdrawal of some of the amniotic fluid which surrounds the fetus; this fluid contains chromosomes that can be studied for the presence of genetic defects. Dozens of genetic disorders, many of them serious, can now be detected with much accuracy by amniocentesis between about the 13th and 18th weeks of pregnancy. Most defects cannot be treated adequately; a common step taken is prevention by abortion.[3]

The question of whether or not to abort the abnormal fetus is a question not just of the value of life of the fetus but of the value of the life of an unhealthy fetus. Does a fetus have less right to life, does it count for less, when it is abnormal? It is interesting that the question is usually answered in terms of the value of health. "For some people, abortion of a defective fetus is less unsavory than abortion of a presumably normal fetus . . . in line with our medical orientation that makes the extirpation of disease a noble act."[4] The decision to abort is made in the interest of health. The point made is not so much that the fetus' life is less valuable because it is abnormal but that we would not be fulfilling our obligations to take care of the health of our children if we did not prevent this diseased child from being born. Selective abortions, more than other abortions, appear to be justified in terms of the benefit to the child himself. The parents would not have had an abortion for other reasons; health is the crucial factor.

Those who oppose selective abortion argue that the interests of a sick person are not served by killing him, that a disease is not prevented by ending someone's life. Our moral obligation is to treat the disease. Abortion is not treatment; we would not ordinarily think much of "therapy" that kills.

The question of selective abortion introduces, then, another dimension of the context in which the deformed infant question is discussed. What is the relationship between our obligations to preserve the lives of those who are under our care and our obligations to keep them healthy and without suffering? This issue, whether to preserve life in the face of suffering, is at the heart of the euthanasia debate. We can now turn to that debate.

*Euthanasia*

There is some indication that euthanasia is replacing abortion as the major ethical issue in medicine and that it is becoming one of the fronts on which legal reformers are hard at work. In some ways, the question of euthanasia may prove to be even more difficult than abortion. Certainly there is much greater confusion regarding exactly what the term means.

The term euthanasia is taken from the Greek and literally means "good death." For some, euthanasia is practiced whenever a decision is made not to attempt to prolong life. For some, euthanasia is practiced only when direct action is taken to end a life to relieve suffering—mercy killing. Sometimes letting the patient die without attempting to extend life is called indirect or passive euthanasia, while actual intervention to bring about death immediately is called direct or active euthanasia. It may very well be that the confusion people experience on this issue is compounded by confusion regarding the use of terms.

The issues can be seen in terms of two questions. First, is it morally acceptable at times to cease all attempts to prolong the life of someone who will die if untreated? Second, when is it morally justifiable to kill a dying patient in order to put an end to his suffering more quickly? While many hold that the differences between the two situations are not great, that both are, in a sense, cases of killing, there are others who insist that there is a vast moral difference between the two. Since it is at least possible to conceive of a serious moral difference between the two types of questions and actions, it may avoid confusion to use different terms. The first might be considered the question of letting someone die and the second the question of mercy killing. We are not considering here the problem of determining whether or not a patient is already dead, but the question of what is the most appropriate way of treating the dying, though alive, patient.

Three major stands being taken on these questions can be discerned:

1. Everything possible must be done to prolong life.
2. Where death should no longer be opposed, it is morally justifiable to let die but not to kill (even mercifully).
3. Where death should no longer be opposed, it is morally justifiable both to let die and to kill mercifully.

According to those who take the first position, neither letting die nor mercy killing is moral. Both involve the notion that death is better than life sometimes, and that is a mistaken notion. Life is good; it is hard to think of a more fundamental or a greater good. To start saying that some lives are no longer worth living because of something like hopelessness or suffering is to start that dangerous process of deciding who shall live and who shall die. Besides, medicine has seen many cases where supposed "hopeless" patients have recovered; until death has occurred there is still hope. It is the duty of the physician to prolong life, not to attempt to decide which life is worth prolonging.

The primary focus of this first position is on the goodness of life. Very little difference is seen between killing somebody directly and letting him die when his life could be extended. In both cases one is responsible for the fact that the person who was previously alive is now dead; his death could have been prevented, at least temporarily. Man does not have the moral right to decide when someone should die. The pursuit of the good demands the constant attempt to extend life. Even the patient himself may not decide that his life is no longer worth living; he, too, has the obligation to protect the life that is there. The avoidance of suffering is a very important goal and ideal, but it is not to be done at the cost of devaluing life itself.

The second position also argues that life is good. In fact, that is precisely the reason that one may never legitimately directly kill an innocent person. The life of a human person is of inherent value, so that even intense pain and imminent death do not justify mercy killing. Even under those conditions, to kill is to violate human life and a human person. Nevertheless, life is not the only good. If the very pursuit of prolonging life begins to destroy other important goods, such as peace of mind, familial responsibilities, and tolerable living conditions, then it may be acceptable to cease the fight to keep death at bay. Life is good, but death may also sometimes be good. Death is natural and inevitable. To accept death at times is not to violate the goodness of life. To directly end life, however, is very different.

Advocates of this second position insist that there is a significant moral difference between killing and letting die—at least in some circumstances. Everyone has a moral obligation to preserve health and extend life, but he does not have to go to extreme lengths. If he does not take ordinary care for his life and health, he is not living up to his obligations. If he dies as a result of not taking ordinary care, it is morally equivalent to killing. But the use of extraordinary means of prolonging life is not demanded. To choose not to use extraordinary means is not the equivalent of killing. It is, rather, letting death occur in order not to harm seriously some other legitimate value. It is the disease or injury that kills in these cases, not a human agent. A classical definition of "ordinary" and "extraordinary" means goes thus:

> *Ordinary* means of preserving life are all medicines, treatments, and operations, which offer a reasonable hope of benefit for the patient and which can be obtained and used without excessive expense, pain, or other inconvenience. . . . *Extraordinary* means of preserving life . . . means all medicines, treatments, and operations, which cannot be obtained without excessive expense, pain or other inconvenience, or which, if used, would not offer a reasonable hope of benefit.[5]

One's obligation to respect the goodness of life is twofold.

He may never directly kill innocent human life; he must use all ordinary means to preserve that life. But life is not an absolute good. If the very means used to attempt to prolong life offer little hope of benefit or if the means involve serious harm to other important dimensions of life, one may choose to let death happen instead. Note, though, that the decision to decline treatment is based more on the implications of the means used then on the quality of the life of the dying person. According to this moral stand, the patient (or family) is not to choose death because suffering makes the life not worth living, but he (or they) may decide against treatment because the *treatment* involves excessive suffering. The difference is not always easy to see, but it means that this position permits death to be unopposed at times while not abandoning its insistence that all lives are of sacred and equal value.

To mercy kill, even for the best of reasons, does not respect the sacred value of life. The end does not justify the means. While the end (purpose) may be good in mercy killing, the means (action taken to achieve the purpose) is unacceptable. It is the very action of mercy killing that violates the goodness of life, no matter what the reason or the circumstances.

The third stand on the euthanasia issue finds letting die and mercy killing both morally acceptable at times. Life is good, but not always. There are times when the conditions of life become such that life is no longer worth living, when those things that human beings cherish most in life have been lost. At these times death is to be preferred. There is no moral difference between letting die by withholding treatment and directly ending life by intervention, except that killing may be more humanitarian if it relieves suffering faster. Both letting die and mercy killing have the same goal or purpose (the best death under the circumstances) and both practices do result in death. The motives are the same, the purposes are the same, and the consequences are the same. Taking that into consideration, the difference between the two types of action has to be considered of little moral consequence.

Human life is good and is never to be considered something of little consequence. But man is most human when he takes control over his own destiny. To say that life is good does not mean that there can never be a time when it is appropriate to intervene to bring about death. Why should one accept the notion, as the second position does, that death can be good only if it is "natural"? That kind of thinking sees the ideal man as one who passively accepts his fate. That is not the image of man that we need. Man is a rational being whose whole life is made more meaningful by the deliberate exercise of control over the type and style of his living and his dying.

When life becomes unbearable because of pain and debility and hopelessness, it is morally acceptable for the patient to take action himself to assure that his life not go on or to request that others help him to a merciful end. It is his moral right to do what he wants with his own body, to exercise rational control over his own destiny.

In addition, mercy killing must be recognized as being *merciful*. We long ago realized that it is better to kill a suffering animal quickly than to let the suffering continue long. Man is not exactly like other animals, of course; he can sometimes rise above suffering or make it an enriching experience—but not always. There are times when suffering is very destructive of the human person. At those times our humanitarian obligation may be to relieve that suffering, even if it means killing. We cannot be less concerned with human suffering than with animal suffering.

The legalization of mercy killing may involve some difficulties, the advocates of this position acknowledge. It is necessary to guard against abuses, so that individuals are not eliminated against their will or because they may be considered socially inferior or because they have unscrupulous relatives. But those abuses can be prevented. The principle on which both the ethics and the laws should be based is the principle that everyone has a right to do what he wants with his own life. It is probably necessary legally to restrict mercy killing to voluntary mercy killing, requested by the patient himself. Other restrictions can also be included if necessary, such as verification of terminal disease. But the point that needs to be recognized is that mercy killing is a morally appropriate way of dealing with terminal suffering at times.

This brief statement of three characteristic positions (they represent, of course, major tendencies and not every conceivable position or defense of position) is sufficient to indicate the real issue at stake. As in the abortion question, the basic issue is the value of life. There the focus was on the value of fetal life; here the question is the value of the life of the suffering and dying person. What does such life count for?

In the first stand, this life counts for everything. There is no justification for killing and no justification for not using every possible means to prolong that life. If we do not protect and extend suffering life, we are beginning to cast doubt on the goodness and inviolability of all human life. Life counts for everything because, in medicine, the fight is against death.

In the second approach, the life of the suffering and dying person also counts for much. But the difference between positions one and two is really quite significant. Here life is of such value that it is not to be taken directly in mercy killing. It is good because it is one of the most fundamental gifts that the world has received, not because death is the enemy. In fact, death also is to be accepted. Human life, even suffering human life, is to be protected from man's own attempt to dominate, but is not to be considered man's possession that is to be fought for at all costs. It is not death that is the enemy, but man's destruction of life or man's neglect of ordinary care of health. What is to be opposed is man's overstepping of bounds or man's not living up to obligations, not nature.

In the third position, suffering life counts for much, but not so much as the right of possession. It is more important to protect the right to do what one wants with one's body and the right to decide for self what constitutes life worth living than it is to protect the fact of life. More important than the fact of life is the type of life being lived; it is more important to relieve suffering than to prolong or protect life. The enemy is not death, but intolerable suffering and life considered not worth living. To resist this enemy, it is necessary to argue that suffering life counts for less than the right to do what one wants with that life.

In addition to considering how much life counts for, we can also look at the euthanasia debate in terms of *how* the different approaches value life. It is possible to distinguish between one view which sees life as a *possession* and another view that sees life as a *gift*.

When life is viewed as a possession, there are no limits to what one may do to it or with it. It is one's own, to be used as the individual sees fit. Life as a possession is something to be controlled and used. When life is seen this way, one is likely to claim the right to destroy that possession for sufficient reasons. Valuing life as a possession goes hand in hand with the defense of mercy killing.

When life is viewed as a gift, on the other hand, there are limits to what one may do to it and with it. To see life as a gift (at least as the term is being used here) means to have an attitude of acceptance and protection rather than of control. Life is not entirely one's own; it will be taken away again. While one has the gift of life, it is not to be violated or abused by oneself or others. The view of life as a gift seems to be closely related to opposition to mercy killing.

There is one way in which the first and third positions are similar. Both tend to see very little moral difference between the practice of letting someone die by withholding treatment and the practice of mercy killing. One is opposed to both while one approves of both, but they agree that the two are very similar morally. The second position, as we saw, holds that there is a very significant moral difference between the two practices. Perhaps the first and third positions differ from the second in the way moral positions are reached. In the third position, something is moral (in the euthanasia context) if being undertaken for the purpose of relieving suffering. In the first position, something is moral if undertaken to prolong life. Both of these ethical orientations seem to focus on the purpose and the immediate consequences of acting. In other words, what does one want to accomplish here and now? In the second position, something is moral if it does not violate the obligations to take ordinary care and not to kill (obligations which are arrived at, often, by concern for long-range consequences). Thus, it is a morality that focuses more on the actions than on the immediate consequences. In a sense, the euthanasia debate is a debate about how one resolves moral problems, a debate between a morality of intentions (what one wants to accomplish) and a morality of actions (what is to be done). A morality of actions can see a big moral difference in different actions (between letting die and killing) even when the immediate consequences are similar. A morality of intentions sees little or no difference in actions when it is known that the consequences will be very similar.

This look at the euthanasia issue has indicated that the seeking of a solution to the question of what constitutes appropriate treatment raises important issues concerning underlying values and assumptions. The value of life is one. Another is the question of one's overall orientation toward life (possession or gift). A third involves one's fundamental ethical orientation (morality of intentions, morality of actions). Values like these are very important in the handicapped infant questions and should be probed more deeply before we can fully appreciate positions on that specific question.

## Value of Life

In an attempt to explain and analyze the different ways in which life is valued in the questions of abortion and euthanasia, two conflicting approaches are sometimes compared. These two have come to be known as the "sanctity of life ethic" and the "quality of life ethic." The sanctity of life ethic holds that every human life is intrinsically good, that no one life is more valuable than another, that lives not yet fully developed (embryonic and fetal stages) and lives with no great potential (the suffering lives of the terminally ill or the pathetic lives of the severely handicapped) are still sacred. The condition of a life does not reduce its value or justify its termination. The quality of life ethic puts the emphasis on the type of life being lived, not upon the fact of life. Lives are not all of one kind; some lives are of great value to the person himself and to others while others are not. What the life means to someone is what is important. Keeping this in mind, it is not inappropriate to say that some lives are of greater value than others, that the condition or meaning of life does have much to do with the justification for terminating that life.

The sanctity of life ethic defends two propositions:

1. That human life is sacred by the very fact of its existence; its value does not depend upon a certain condition or perfection of that life.
2. That, therefore, all human lives are of equal value; all have the same right to life.

The quality of life ethic finds neither of these two propositions acceptable. Things are valuable when they are of value to someone; life is good when it is meaningful to someone, especially to that person himself. The mere fact of life does not immediately mean that life is good or sacred. Thus, ending one type of human life is not always of the same moral nature as ending another type.

The sanctity of life ethic has acknowledged that there may be times when it is morally acceptable to directly kill someone. Traditionally, killing has been recognized as legitimate in self-defense against unjust aggression, in participation in a just war (criteria have been developed to help determine which wars are just and which are not), in capital punishment, and—according to some—in tyrannicide (when an illegitimate and unjust ruler can be removed in no other way). In all four of these cases, killing is justified because the one being killed has, by his actions, forfeited his right to life. Killing is not permitted because the lives of some are considered less valuable than the lives of others. Rather, it is permitted only because of the actions taken. This, it is argued, is not a quality of life judgment, but one based on more objective criteria, what the person is doing or has done. When the aggressive actions that forfeit the right to life have not been taken, there is no justification for killing, no matter what the condition of someone's life. Innocent human life may never be directly taken.

Some who are within the sanctity of life tradition think that the tradition may have gone too far in recognizing the legitimacy of killing (as in capital punishment). Others think that the whole emphasis should not be placed on innocence or injustice (as when an innocent fetus threatens the mother's life). But all within the sanctity of life school agree that the killing cannot be justified because someone's life is seen as less valuable on the basis of its condition; killing can only be justified in response to actions which threaten life.

The sanctity of life ethic and the quality of life ethic are not totally exclusive. The sanctity of life ethic is concerned with quality, with the type of life that is being lived. Advocates of this position insist, however, that "if each and every life is not accorded full worth and equality, then the quality of the whole of society will be seriously endangered."[6] The quality of life ethic is not unconcerned with the value of life itself. Advocates of this position maintain, however, that it is impossible to make responsible moral decisions in individual situations if we always place an absolute prohibition on taking innocent life. Placing such absolute value on life is "thoroughly idolatrous"[7] and does not give us the opportunity to give due consideration to other factors. The two positions are not totally exclusive, but their orientations are so different that they disagree on many practical issues.

It is, in fact, precisely these underlying differences in the way life is valued that accounts for much of the disagreement on abortion and euthanasia. Those who emphasize the very fact of life as being the basis for its value (the sanctity school) feel an obligation to respect life totally as soon as it is present. Though life in the early stages of pregnancy is not fully developed, it is life of the human species and, as such, needs to be protected against direct destruction. Its condition does not diminish its value. Those who emphasize the condition and meaning of life (the quality school) feel an obligation to recognize that the woman's life is, at present, of much greater value. She may be justified, therefore, to end the life within in defense of a certain value in her own life. She may also be justified in having an abortion to guard against a life of poor quality for the child who would be born or for other members of the family or society. The obligation to try to bring about a good life for all concerned is more important than the obligation to protect undeveloped human life.

In the case of mercy killing, the sanctity of life ethic insists that as long as a person is alive, direct killing is always an unjustified attack upon the sacredness of life. This is true even when the killing is requested by the patient himself, because the value of life does not depend upon how much meaning that life has for the individual or for anyone else. It should be noted very carefully, though, that the sanctity of life ethic does *not* insist that everything possible must be done to prolong life in all cases; it is not opposed to the practice of withholding or ceasing treatment at times. That does not directly attack the goodness of life; it recognizes that death is natural and that life is not the only good to be concerned with. But direct killing of an innocent person always violates the goodness of life. The quality of life ethic finds it morally responsible at times to mercy kill because the obligation to avoid a meaningless and severely painful life is greater than the obligation to protect life simply because it is human.

It is something of an oversimplification to suggest that all the ways in which men value human life can be placed in either one of these two categories. This author has elsewhere suggested one way in which the scheme might be refined to include a position that can be called "the sanctity of personal life ethic."[8] This approach argues that all human lives are sacred and of equal value provided they are capable of personal living. The life that is to be considered sacred is not to be identified with biological life of the human species; it is personal life that is sacred. In a sense, then, this position rejects the first but accepts a variation of the second of the sanctity of life propositions.

Some such refinement (and probably others as well) would seem to be necessary to give full justice to the positions that are taken on the value of life. For our purposes here, though, the basic distinction between the sanctity of life and the quality of

life positions is sufficient to indicate the fundamental importance of the very way in which persons view life. For many
(sanctity), man's obligations are determined by the fact of life
and justification for killing has to be based on the objective
criteria of actions. For many others (quality) man's obligations
are determined by what things mean to persons and justification
of killing has to be based on the value that life has for persons.
These are two fundamentally different ways of viewing moral
obligations. A more careful consideration of these ethical
worldviews will help us to understand why people take the
moral stands that they do.


*Ethical Worldviews*

When we get back to one's fundamental ethical orientation
we are dealing with the very way in which he sees things as having meaning and value. This is what is being described here as
an ethical worldview—one's universe of meaning and value and
man's place in that universe.

Recognizing that this involves the same danger of oversimplification as the sanctity of life-quality of life distinction,
but recognizing as well that it involves the same usefulness in indicating underlying differences, I would like to describe in the
following pages two characteristic ethical worldviews which are
behind and shaping the different responses to abortion and euthanasia. It is precisely because they tend toward one or the other
of these understandings of man's moral obligations that individuals tend to accept or reject abortion and mercy killing.

Both worldviews have existed side by side for centuries.
One, however, seems to have been the predominant one in the
past while the other has been becoming increasingly common in
recent times. We can call the first the "classical" or "traditional" worldview and the second the "modern." Both are very
much alive today. People are not always able to articulate their
own worldviews and they are often not conscious of them, but
some such orientation underlies their position-taking.

In the classical worldview, man, both as the race and as the individual, is seen as being a very important part of the universe but he is not at the very center. The world has meaning and value apart from the meaning and value given to it by man. Man's own life, too, has a given meaning and purpose. His moral obligations are to accept, respect, and live in accordance with that meaning and purpose.

To determine what is a morally correct mode of behavior, an individual must attempt to discover the duties and obligations which the given meaning of things imposes upon him. In this classical worldview, the tendency is to stress moral obligations rather than moral rights. The focus is not on the individual, but on the larger context to which the individual must respond. The primary obligation may be expressed in terms of doing the will of God which is largely expressed in the created order of things. Or it may be expressed in terms of one's need to be in tune with nature. Or it may be expressed in terms of responsibility toward fellowmen. But, in any of these expressions, the emphasis is placed on the obligation of the individual to respond. He does not give meaning; he must respect the meaning already present.

For someone of the classical mentality, the starting point of moral analysis is rational reflection. What would the contemplated action involve? What are its implications? Is it in conformity with the obligation to respect the goodness and order of creation? Individual situations and individual differences are not stressed; first it is necessary to understand what any action of this sort involves. By withdrawing slightly from the situation and reflecting upon the larger context, it is possible to draw up guidelines to be followed which indicate one's obligations. To begin the decision-making process by dwelling on the circumstances of an individual case is to court the danger of deciding what is of immediate benefit to the individual rather than deciding what the individual must do to respect a common good. An abortion decision can be made pretty clearly once and for all and does not need to be begun anew in each individual case. A careful analysis of what abortion involves reveals that this is an unjustifiable destruction of human life. Man's obligation is to respect life, to be willing to undergo some suffering in defense of life, and to accept responsibility for his sexual behavior. To resort to the violence of innocent life-taking to solve problems (even serious problems) is contrary to the obligation to protect what is given us to protect. The classical view sees life as a gift, not as a possession.

The ability to decide the morality of questions without focusing on individual cases indicates another characteristic of the classical worldview. Morality is to be understood as a morality of actions rather than (or at least more than) a morality of intentions. Abortion is abortion whether the desire is to avoid a deformity or to not interrupt a career. Abortion is still direct assault upon helpless human life. The intention to abort so that the child will not have to suffer is much more admirable than the intention to abort to avoid an inconvenience, but the intention is not the most important factor. To put too much emphasis on intention is to stress what the action means to the *persons* involved, not how the action affects the right ordering of things that man is bound to respect. Actions have more impact upon the conditions of life than intentions do.

The classical ethical worldview, in summary:

1. The world has meaning apart from the meaning given by man.
2. The individual must *discover* what is the right thing to do.
3. The focus in morality is on the action.
4. The moral obligations of the individual are stressed.
5. The starting point of moral analysis is rational reflection on the nature and implications of actions.
6. Life is a gift.

This leads, in medical ethics, to what has previously been described as the sanctity of life ethic. Human life is good in and of itself; its value does not depend upon what it means to persons.

The relationship between the classical worldview and opposition to mercy killing can be clearly recognized. Because the facts of life are to be accepted and respected, man should accept but not attempt to control death. Because actions are very important morally, there is a sharp moral difference between letting die and killing. Because the emphasis is placed on the general moral obligation and not on individual differences, the suffering of the individual or the hopelessness of the situation is not decisive. Because the end does not justify the means, the fact that the killing is done in mercy does not justify it.

The modern ethical worldview puts much more emphasis on the role of man. Man's role is largely to exercise dominion over the world; man is at or near the center of the universe of meaning and value. Whatever meaning there may be apart from man is not so important as the meaning given by man. Man's moral obligations are not to be defined so much in terms of acceptance and respect as in terms of the need to be compassionate and wise as he exercises control. For the world is what man will make of it, man is what man will make of himself, and the responsibility is to make the world as good a one as possible for humankind.

When an individual is making a moral decision, he should begin by recognizing that there are a variety of options open to him. None of these possibilities should be rejected out of hand. He is free to choose any one of them. Right conduct is not something that is imposed from outside. What is right is to be decided by the individual, who should pick that option which is most likely to meet the needs of the individual and his fellowmen. The focus in morality has to be placed on the "end," the purpose for which an action is undertaken. Man is answerable to himself in morality; he should be expected to do neither more nor less than what, according to his best insight, constitutes an action calculated to do good for persons.

According to the modern worldview, the nature of man and the universe does not impose specific moral obligations. There are no universal moral laws and any guidelines that have been developed are to be used with discrimination. Generally speaking, killing of human persons is wrong. But what about this particular case? Whether killing is right or wrong in this case depends upon the nature of the case, the alternatives, and the probable consequences. Morality must be somewhat individualistic and situational. What is right in one case may not be right in another. Since there is no, objectively speaking, "right" answer to questions of morality, the moral freedom of the individual to decide for himself must be stressed.

As the individual begins his moral analysis, he tends to consult his own experience and perception. What would this action mean for me, in this situation? In an abortion situation, for example, the emphasis is placed on the reasons why an abortion is being considered. It is the best solution to this particular situation that is being sought. Whatever action is chosen is moral as long as it is truly selected as most conducive to the perceived good of those involved.

The modern ethical worldview, in summary:

1. The world is largely meaningless until given meaning by man.
2. The individual must *decide* for himself what is the right thing to do.
3. The focus in morality is on the purpose of the action.
4. The moral freedom and rights of the individual are stressed.
5. The starting point of moral analysis is the experience and perception of individuals.
6. Life is a possession.

The modern worldview involves the attitude that has been discussed as the quality of life ethic. The value of life depends on what it means to someone. Unqualified value cannot be placed upon anything, including human life; it all depends upon the situation.

The modern worldview provides the basis for support of mercy killing. Because it is man's role to exercise dominion over the world, he has a right to exercise control over life and death. Because the morality of an action depends primarily upon the reasons for which it is done, mercy killing is no more evil than withholding treatment in the care of a dying patient. Because individuals are not bound by moral rules, the maxim not to kill an innocent person does not mean that such killing is never justified. Because his moral analysis begins with his individual experience of the situation, he cannot abstract from the suffering and hopelessness of the individual case.

It is possible for both the classical worldview and the modern worldview to be associated with religious faith and with the moral absolute that man must always attempt to do the will of God. But the religious understandings are different. For the classicalist, the moral will of God is identical with his created will. The will of God for man is largely expressed in the natural ordering of creation. Man's obligation is to use his reasoning to come to know what is (what the purpose is) so that he can act out of respect for and in accordance with that created meaning. The modernist sees man's relationship to God and the world somewhat differently. God has created man to exercise dominion over creation. His moral obligation is to use the reason God has given him to fashion a world which is better for man. Creation does not impose moral obligations; it has been given by God as the material with which and the context within which to exercise responsible freedom.

It may be necessary to remind the reader that these two worldviews are artificial constructs. They constitute an attempt on the author's part to help explain some of the underlying differences in orientation that account for the different positions taken on specific issues. A typology of this sort should be used when helpful; no attempt should be made to force the views of individuals into an artificial mold. Most moralists and most citizens, I would suggest, tend toward one or the other of these sets of moral assumptions, though there are probably very few pure types.

Debates on life and death issues in recent years in America have often seen one side accusing the other of a fundamental contradiction. It has been fairly common for support for the American participation in the war in Vietnam to go hand in hand with opposition to abortion. Opponents have been quick to criticize: How can you claim that abortion destroys the sanctity of life while advocating killing in Vietnam? On the other hand, support for abortion has often been accompanied by opposition to the war. This combination has also been criticized as insupportable: How can you say that the war is wrong when you defend the killing of the helpless here at home?

The classical-modern discussion may serve to clarify these positions (without claiming that either is totally consistent). Both become quite understandable when placed in the larger context of how ethical decisions are made.

The anti-war, pro-abortion stand can be related to the modern worldview. The primary focus is not on the actual act of killing, whether the question be war or abortion. The Vietnam war is seen as wrong because it imposed suffering without corresponding benefits and because young men were forced to serve whether they wanted to or not. News coverage of the war made it possible to experience, in a removed but real way, the suffering of the Vietnamese and of the American soldiers. Opposition to the war was thus based upon such goals as the relieving of suffering and the defense of freedom. Support for abortion is often the result of the same motives and goals. The woman's right to control her own body and the prevention of suffering can both be goals that inspire support for abortion. The fetus' suffering and death in abortion is something that is very hard to identify with, much harder than it is to identify with the suffering of a Vietnamese peasant thousands of miles away. The combination of an anti-war and pro-abortion stand does not strike one as so contradictory when seen as an expression of the modern worldview. If this stand is to be criticized, the criticism probably has to be directed toward the underlying worldview.

The pro-war, anti-abortion stand is sometimes taken by persons who represent the classical worldview. It is innocent human life that may never be directly taken. War can sometimes be justified, especially in defense against aggression. One's moral obligations include the pursuit of individual freedom and relief from suffering, but a more basic obligation is to protect innocent human life, both the lives of human fetuses and the lives of those being unjustly warred upon. Over the centuries, the sanctity of life tradition has recognized that war can sometimes be justified while abortion cannot; the contemporary pro-war, anti-abortion stand reflects this tradition. Some who approach these questions from a classical orientation have found themselves in opposition both to war and to abortion. To them this war was not one of those that could be justified; it is not clear that Americans were defending the innocent against the unjust. But the actual working out of the classical tradition has made it possible for many to support killing in war while opposing abortion. Criticism of the pro-war, anti-abortion stand should probably be directed primarily toward the sanctity of life tradition and its historical development.

The assumptions, attitudes, and values that are at work in the formation of abortion and euthanasia positions are the very same assumptions, attitudes, and values that are shaping positions on the question of whether to treat severely handicapped infants. This has to be kept in mind as we take positions. Whatever response we give to an individual question not only reflects but also contributes to one of the fundamental ethical orientations. That kind of contribution should only be made with eyes open. Its implications for the future may be tremendously important.

We are now ready to examine some of the different stands being taken on the morality of not treating severely handicapped infants.

# 3
# The Debate

In analyzing the debate on the proper moral response to the plight of the severely handicapped infant, it is best to consider two levels. The first is the debate that is taking place among interested persons who are not professionally trained in the traditions and science of ethics. This may involve parents, medical personnel, lawyers, legislators, editorial writers, members of special interest groups, and other interested individuals. They are attempting to find the best moral solution to the problem and to arrive at a practical manner of resolving the dilemma. As is to be expected, there are major disagreements.

The other level is the discussion of the issue by professional ethicists. Their concern is to analyze the ethical dimensions and to propose ways of resolving the problem that reflect the moral wisdom of their particular traditions and that reflect, as well, a compassionate application of guidelines that should regulate all human interaction. Their role is, in a sense, to be the moral "experts" in society, to provide some of the detailed analyses of moral dimensions of procedures that others do not have the opportunity to make themselves. On the severely handicapped infant issue, there is also much disagreement among professional ethicists.

It is very important to examine the debate at both levels. To consider only the views of the "experts" is to fail to realize that public moral thinking provides the only sound context within which ethicists should offer their views. Ethicists are naturally very aware of what other ethicists are saying, and unless they frequently turn their attention to the actual moral values of other members of society, they may not be aware of the implications of their own ideas. There is always the tendency to have a particular conversation partner in mind, an "opponent," as one outlines his proposals. What one decides needs to be recognized and stressed is precisely what that "opponent" is neglecting or undervaluing. Thus, the choice of "opponent" in an ethical debate is very important. To make sure that the choice is a wise one, ethicists need to be very much aware of the actual moral thinking of the larger society. That is the thinking upon which, ultimately, they want to have an impact. We, therefore, need to examine some common moral positions in our society before we can properly evaluate the contributions of ethicists.

If, on the other hand, we consider only the debate that is taking place among the "non-experts," we will miss an opportunity to hear some carefully reasoned analyses that have been made by ethicists. It is difficult to determine how much of a direct impact the teaching and writing of "experts" has on the moral decisions of individuals, but there can be no doubt that they contribute to the moral climate in which individual decision are made. For a full understanding of the moral dimensions of the questions that we are considering, and for possible new insight into how the situation might be handled, it is necessary to consider the arguments of several representative ethicists.

This chapter consists primarily of giving attention to the views of others. Criticisms are not made, not yet. First it is necessary to see what people are actually thinking; then we can choose more wisely the "opponents" that need to be criticized and the emphasis that needs to be placed in our own efforts to arrive at a just solution.

## Conflicting Primary Values

Close attention to the discussions that have been taking place among individuals reveals a variety of moral approaches to the question of whether severely handicapped infants should survive. Very often problems of this sort are discussed in terms of one particular concern, one particular value, that means a great deal to the individual. It is to protect this primary value that a certain position is taken. In the debate among non-ethicists, a number of primary values are being defended. Let us listen to that debate.

The first speaker's primary value could probably be described as *the least possible suffering*. His argument might go something like the following. "I think that there are definitely times when it would be better for a baby of this sort to die quickly. I am distressed at all the unnecessary suffering that could be prevented if these children would not survive. Some live for years in institutions but never develop beyond the diaper stage. Others live at home with their families, with the result that none of the members of the family can have a normal life. There is no need for this. There is no need to keep an abnormal baby alive. That is not practicing compassionate medicine.

"It is important that we realize that we must act to relieve suffering whenever possible. It is the only humanitarian thing to do. If medicine is practiced without constant awareness of the suffering that may result from intervention or non-intervention, then it is a technology that has been divorced from its human element.

"It would be immoral to plan to have a child if you knew that there was a very great chance that the child would be seriously diseased. The same thing is true once the child is born. A seriously defective child, with no hope of radical improvement, should not be treated. If it does not die quickly, it might even be better to help it die. I'm not sure about that. Killing is a terrible thing—but to kill to relieve suffering is not the same as killing out of malice. Above all, we have to remember the types of lives these children will live and the suffering they will endure."

Another voice in the debate is that of the person whose primary value is *the protection of life*. "What distresses me is the audacity of those who suggest that we decide who lives or who dies. What right do we have to make such decisions? Who has made us judge of what constitutes life worth saving and what does not? Life is precious. Look at the way all of us hang on to ours. How can we think that these infants do not want their lives? We who bring these children into the world have an obligation to protect those lives if we can.

"I am not unaware of the problems these children and their families face. It is difficult, most difficult. But the alternative is much worse. Just try to imagine what things will be like if it becomes established policy that parents can decide which of their children will live and which will die. It's bad enough that this can happen with abortion. If we cannot draw the line at birth, will we be able to draw the line anywhere? To be parents is to have the privilege and obligation of caring for new life. Whether that baby has the potential to be an average, normal person, or whether that baby has the potential to be a genius or a great leader, or whether that baby has only the potential to be a retarded, deformed child makes no difference. Our obligation is to protect that life which we are responsible for and which is of such fundamental value."

The debate goes on. The-least-possible-suffering ethic and the-protection-of-life ethic are two of the most common stances taken. But there are a variety of others that also need to be heard.

Those whose primary value is *the welfare of society* are also speaking. "We are living in a society in which there are limited resources, both medical and social. In establishing policy for the care of handicapped infants, we have to keep in mind the fact that treatment involves using resources that may be more needed elsewhere. Think of the mental energy, the money, and the other resources that could be used for those whose lives can really be helped, if we do not use them on these children in hospitals and institutions. We have to think of the question in the context of the larger society. Where can we best use our resources, so that the common good is best served? We have to use them where there is most likelihood of getting some benefit. Nothing else makes sense.

"These infants, even with the best of treatment, are always to be unproductive or nearly so. All the effort that the family and society put into caring for these kids comes to nothing, in a sense; they will never be able to do their part, to make their contributions. It may sound a little hardhearted, but we have to be practical. Those who are productive in our society are carrying all the burdens of job responsibilities and taxes and so on. What we need is a higher percentage of those contributing to the welfare of society, not of those living off the work of others.

"I am not suggesting that someone's life is only worth living if he is productive. I am not saying that the rest of us should not assume responsibility for someone who is unable to do productive work. Of course we should. But, at the same time, we should be practical. If an infant is born with a serious abnormality so that he will always be a social liability, then it may very well be best if he not survive."

From time to time another voice is raised in the debate, the voice of those who approach the issue in terms of *the survival of the fittest*. "It is not too difficult for one who has learned nature's own solution to resolve this moral dilemma. Nature's way is simple: those that are healthy survive; those that are not, do not. It is the weak and diseased among the caribou that the wolves feed on; the healthy are in no great danger. There is some evidence that some animal mothers destroy their own babies if they are misshapen. And, of course, our knowledge of evolutionary development has taught us very clearly that the same thing is true in the long run—only the fittest survive. We can learn a very important lesson from nature. The world belongs to the healthy, and we are doing ourselves and our descendants no service by striving so diligently to keep alive the unfit.

"Many people are turned off by the 'survival of the fittest' talk concerning human affairs. They think of me and those who agree with me as monsters who are proposing that we live according to the 'law of the jungle.' They have not come to see that sound scientific knowledge must be at the basis of ethics. Now that we know about evolution and about nature's way of handling the handicapped, we can develop an ethical approach that makes use of that knowledge. Cruel as it may sound to say it, soft-hearted morality is mistaken. It does not pay enough attention to the consequences. We have to think in the long-range terms of man's evolutionary development. To spend our lives keeping alive the deformed and unhealthy will, in the long run, do harm to the race. The science of genetics is making that point perfectly clear. To keep someone alive now may contribute to the weakening of the race down the line.

"A good place to start with a scientific ethic is with severely handicapped infants. There it is easy to see our moral obligation   they should not survive. We do not need to feel bad about the death of such infants or about our decision that results in their death. They could only weaken the race; the decision that they die is well founded."

A voice that rings out loud and clear in many discussions of morality today is the voice of those whose primary value is *the freedom of conscience.* "I think I know what I would do if I had to make the decision about one of these babies, but I cannot tell someone else what is right for him or her. I wouldn't want anyone else to impose his position on me and I will not impose my position on someone else. The most important thing is that everyone be left free to decide for himself what is the right thing to do. So I really cannot say if or when it is right not to treat abnormal babies; I can only say what I would do. Morality is basically a matter of opinion and each person has to act according to his or her own opinion.

"In line with my desire that no one impose a moral position on another person, I would like to see the policies that are established to regulate the situation allow as much freedom as possible. I can support the parents who do everything possible to keep their baby alive; I can support the parents who withhold treatment and let their baby die; I can also support the parents who kill their baby because it can never have a meaningful life. I can support any of these decisions as long as the parents are deciding according to their own best consciences. What is morally right is what those who have to make the decision think is morally right. There is no such thing as the *right* answer. It all depends on the situation and on those involved. At all costs, we have to avoid imposing one person's morality on someone else."

A final speaker who might be listened to in this debate among conflicting primary values is the one who focuses on *sufficient mental capacity.* "We should do what we can to treat newborn babies who are suffering from physical deformities, but I am not so sure we should do so when the child is always going to be mentally retarded. A child with a physical handicap has much to suffer but, if he is mentally normal, he can still enjoy a rich human life. Someone who is seriously retarded, however, may never even know what he is missing; he simply is not able to live the type of life that we understand to be the way a human person lives. When the prognosis for an infant is that he or she will never be able to have much mental ability, there seems little reason to take any steps to preserve that life. What for?

"The question of whether the handicapped child should be helped to survive after birth should be answered on the basis of a careful estimation of future mental capacity. It is hard, of course, to draw the line but I would suggest that the line be drawn at about the point of educability. If it is likely that the child will be educable, that he or she will be able to acquire some minimum mental skills (such as very basic reading), then I would treat the child. If the child is not likely to ever rise above the mental level of three years or so, then it would be better for the baby to die right away. That is no kind of life; one is simply not meant to be a mental baby all his life."

These six voices reveal some of the most important starting points from which people advance toward a solution to this problem. What can be said about these primary values? Much will have to be said later, as this author's own position will have to take account of these arguments. Only a couple of preliminary observations need to be made here.

While hearing this conversation, one might have noted that two different types of arguments are used. Three of the approaches (least possible suffering, protection of life, sufficient mental capacity) argue that the decision about survival should be made primarily, if not exclusively, on the basis of the quality or value of that child's life itself. The decision is not to be based on how others will be affected (except perhaps how they might be affected if attention is not focused on this individual's life). The social impact is neither decisive nor primary. The other three arguments (welfare of society, survival of fittest, and freedom of conscience) place the emphasis on the social context. The decision should be made largely on the basis of the impact upon society. The difference, then, is basically between those who want to decide the question in terms of the child's own interest (as they see it) and those who want to decide the question in terms of society's interest (as they see it). We will have to decide which of these is a sounder approach and why.

Another observation is that most of these six primary values could have many other applications besides to the handicapped infant situation. It has been predicted by some that we are rapidly approaching some very difficult times, when we will be faced with severe problems of overpopulation, of food shortages, of continued energy shortages, of economical crises, of conflicts between the "haves" and the "have nots" of the world, etc.[1] If these predictions are even partly correct, we will be faced with many problems that need quick action. Think what kind of attempts may be made to resolve these problems if the decision is made on the basis of some of the primary values we have here seen advocated. Would these solutions be desirable?

The moral stand one takes on the deformed infant question can never be totally isolated from other issues; the soundest moral approach will contribute not only to an acceptable resolution of this problem but also to a total value system that will lead to acceptable solutions to other major problems as they emerge.

Among the many individuals considering the most appropriate management of the handicapped infant cases, most have not been trained in ethics. They argue in ways that have been presented here—and in some other ways as well. Stepping into this discussion are a number of ethicists, well acquainted with moral theories and their applications. Let us see what they have to say.

*Representative Ethicists*

Among those ethicists who have addressed themselves to the questions of if and when there is legitimate reason not to work for the survival of the severely handicapped infant, four have been selected to be considered here. A careful look at the positions of these four individuals will provide insight into the nature of the debate among ethicists.

David Smith reflected "On Letting Some Babies Die" in *The Hastings Center Studies*, in May of 1974.[2] His primary conclusions are stated thus:

> In summary, I regard withholding treatment from defective newborns as wrong unless (1) it can be argued that the action is necessary to protect the personal life of at least one specifiable other person or (2) the infant cannot receive care in any other form. This amounts to a prohibition of active or passive infanticide on most newborns. I am uneasy with this conclusion, although I cannot see my way clear to any other.[3]

Smith can find only two situations that would justify killing a newborn child or letting him die. Neither of these situations is likely to be found more than rarely. For all practical purposes, then, there is no justification of these procedures. This does not necessarily mean for Smith that everything possible must be done to prolong these lives as far as possible. But *something* must be done; we should not withhold treatment entirely so that the baby will die.

An act of killing (or of letting someone die untreated—Smith appears to see little moral difference between the two) might be considered morally correct for either of two reasons. We might be justified in killing someone as a way of saving or protecting the life of someone else. This is the type of argument that has often been used to explain why killing in warfare is sometimes called for. Or we might be justified in killing as a way of doing good to the one who is dying. This is the type of argument often used to explain why euthanasia is called for.

As Smith sees it, the argument for killing a handicapped newborn as a way of protecting others is not convincing, at least not in foreseeable cases. The moral tradition has recognized that more is needed to support killing in war than the fact that such killing is a defense of the lives or welfare of others. Additional conditions have been made to ensure that life not be taken lightly. Two of the conditions are that war be engaged in only after due process has been observed and only as a last resort, there being no other alternative way of protecting people. While it is true that an abnormal child does pose a threat to the welfare of others, especially the family, the threat is usually not an immediate threat to the very personhood of some individual. Nor is there usually the absence of other alternative forms of protection. Nor have procedures been established to assure infants of some semblance of due process. Under these circumstances, the argument for killing such an infant (or letting him die) in order to protect others is not convincing.

There may be times when one is justified in killing another in the interest of the one being killed. "One decides for his death because, in his case, such a decision is better for him."[4] Such a case exists when someone cannot receive care in any other form, as when he is dying and nothing can any longer be done to prevent that dying or when he is permanently unconscious. In such situations, there is good reason for ceasing attempts to prolong life and for simply caring for the person as he dies or even, perhaps, for killing him directly. For Smith, such an argument might be used to defend euthanasia. But it demands a decision that this particular person is beyond our ability to care for him in any other way. It is precisely this decision that cannot ordinarily be made of newborns. We have, as yet, no opportunity to know the normality of the functioning of this particular person. "Thus, in the absence of a benchmark in past life for saying *this particular person* has started to die, I do not see how one committed to care . . . could ever switch from cure to companionship. The yardsticks which would give such a decision provisional legitimacy in the case of an adult (that is, consent and/or establishment of a norm of life) are absent in the case of the newborn. In their absence we should not disjoin care and cure."[5]

For Smith, therefore, our moral obligation in the case of newborns is to attempt to cure, regardless of the condition of that life. He argues that this obligation does not mean always doing everything possible to cure, but doing something in an attempt to cure. It may very well be an unwise use of our limited resources to do everything possible for handicapped infants. If we cannot adequately treat all because of limited resources, that cannot be helped. But we have an obligation to treat those whom it is within our power to help. "The error we want to avoid is the notion that we should solve our limited resource problem simply by assessing the 'quality' of the output. Such an approach leads one to think that the ideal result is either a 'perfect' baby or a dead baby. And the root problems of this way of looking at the issue are that both the human rights of defectives and the imperfections of all babies are glossed over."[6]

Thus David Smith comes down against the practice of letting deformed infants die by withholding treatment. That is killing, and the killing of human persons is only morally defensible in very limited situations. It may, for example, be proper to kill to protect the lives of others. It may be proper to kill someone who is totally without capability of receiving love, who is beyond human care. But since neither of these situations is clearly present in the case of a handicapped infant, we must treat him as an expression of our obligation to care for him.

One of the most widely known ethicists in the country, Joseph Fletcher, argues a very different position. Fletcher insists that at times it is proper to bring about the death of a severely retarded baby; in fact, no other course of action could be considered responsible in some circumstances. Fletcher has probably most clearly articulated his position on the question in his commentary on the father's plea that children with Down's syndrome be administered death, a plea quoted in the first chapter of this work. What follows is a statement of the main points Fletcher made at that time.

As Fletcher sees it, our laws and the moral thinking of many people make an idol of life. Too often the tendency is to "absolutize mere biological life."[7] Such an idolatrous and vitalistic approach to life is seriously mistaken. In the first place, not all life born of woman is human life. Secondly, even true human life is not always good; taking that life is not always an evil.

A human person is not present just because the body is alive. To be a human is to be self-aware, consciously related to others, capable of rationality in a measure at least sufficient to support some initiative. When these things are absent, or cannot ever come to be, there is neither a potential nor an actual person. To be a person is a lot more than just to be alive —as any student of the human struggle for maturity and well-being knows perfectly well. The fact that a biological organism functions biologically does not mean that it is a human being.[8]

There is no reason why anyone should feel any moral guilt about killing a Down's syndrome baby. "True guilt arises only from an offense against a person, and a Down's is not a person."[9] There may be some cause for regret, but none for remorse or true guilt. Infants who will never be capable of truly human functions are not human persons and it is not killing a human person to kill them.

Life, even when it is truly human life, is not an absolute good. It is not an intrinsic good, good in and of itself. Life, like every other value, is good—if and when it is—because of the circumstances. There are times when, because of circumstances, human life is not good. And "when it is not good, it deserves neither protection nor preservation."[10] It is sometimes good to kill, depending on the situation. "Compared to some things, the taking of life is a small evil, and compared to some things, the loss of life is a small evil."[11]

Man's moral responsibility in the face of life-and-death questions is to exercise rational control. Much of our society has adopted a fatalistic attitude; we say that life is God's to give and take, not ours. The idea that we should make no attempts to control life and death is not a Christian or biblical idea. If we took seriously the idea that God was directly at work in all natural phenomena, "all science, including medicine, would die away because we would be afraid to . . . tamper with His activity. Such beliefs are a hopelessly primitive kind of God-thought and God-talk. . . ."[12]

An act can be moral only if humanly chosen. There is no moral value in sitting by fatalistically and letting something happen. We cannot really talk about moral value if something

happens without human control or decision. If, in the mongoloid case, the baby's life "had been brought mercifully to a
close, that would have had ethical value; but with its sudden end
by 'heart failure and jaundice,' neither his life nor his death had
any moral meaning whatsoever."[13] It is the human decision that
gives moral value to something.

Fletcher, like Smith, sees little moral difference between
letting a handicapped child die by withholding treatment and
killing him directly. It is the goal or purpose that gives an act its
moral character, its meaning. Both letting die and killing have
the same purpose; they are of the same moral character.
Fletcher adds, though, that many times direct killing is better
than letting die. It is more straightforward and responsible. To
will the death but not the action of killing to bring that death
about is "dishonest or phony."[14] Keeping in mind that one is
acting most responsibly when he exercises control and does not
wait in resignation for things to occur, it is usually better, once
death is seen as desirable, to act for that end than to merely
wait for it to happen.

Joseph Fletcher, then, not only supports decisions not to
treat infants at times; he also argues that they should, in those
cases, be directly killed. Being very concerned to recognize situational differences and to defend individual freedom, he gives
no clear-cut rules on when exactly death is to be recognized as
better than life for infants. He does, however, give two general
guidelines for the decision. The first is that decisions about
those who are severely retarded mentally are not decisions
about human persons at all. To kill in such cases is not to kill a
human person. Fletcher's second general guideline is that even
when a life is clearly human and clearly innocent of aggressive
behavior, there can be no absolute prohibition against taking
that life. Human lives are of relative value and the circumstances (such as the extent of suffering and the desire to be merciful) might justify a parental decision to kill a deformed child
even if not severely retarded.

There is plenty of ground between the positions taken by
Smith and Fletcher. That ground is not open; it is occupied by
others, two of whom can be looked at here.

Warren Reich takes the position that there is, in some cases, a moral difference between withholding treatment (even though the baby dies as a result) and directly killing. Letting die may be proper at times; killing is not. He disagrees with Smith's contention that every child must be treated. He disagrees as well with Fletcher's argument that some lives are not as human or as valuable as others.

Reich has commented on the "Missy" case that is found in the first chapter of this book. He states his position in this way:

> I believe that in some instances "extraordinary means" may be omitted in pediatric care, even if this means the newborn will die. This means that, in a case such as Missy's, full and adequate treatment should normally be given the newborn, but that in some instances, when the prognosis is very poor, it may legitimately be decided that surgery and other subsequent exceptional treatment should not be performed, and that only supportive care be given.[15]

The moral obligations of parents (and others) regarding the newborn are the same whether the infant is terribly deformed or perfectly normal. We must accept a basic responsibility to care for children and we must acknowledge that we do not have the moral right to put an end to those lives. On the other hand, we do not have an obligation to do everything possible, no matter how heroic the measure or how excessive the pain, to prolong life. "Ethically speaking, the decision of parents and physician does not assume that they have full and prior dominion over the life of the newborn. Rather, their decision is rightly focused only on the feasibility (or non-feasibility) of a certain kind of care, in light of the expected consequences of the treatment."[16]

The obligation to extend human life is not without limits: "Sustaining human life is a good but not an absolute good."[17] When the limits of reasonable efforts are reached, we are then justified in withholding treatment and letting the individual die of his disease or injury. This is proper ethical procedure for an adult who is dying. It is also proper ethical procedure regarding a newborn who is dying. It is not the simple fact that this is letting die rather than killing (an omission rather than a commission) that makes this course of action acceptable at times. A decision to let die when ordinary means could sustain life is as morally repugnant as a decision to kill outright. But the use of a treatment that involves excessive cost, excessive pain, or no reasonable hope of success is different. To see the use of these extraordinary means as morally obligatory is to place the very highest value on the maintenance of life itself, which would be contrary to the Christian ethical tradition.

In addition to the fact that the ordinary means-extraordinary means distinction recognizes a reasonable limit to the obligation to sustain life, it also provides a basis for making decisions about who should live and who should die on objective considerations regarding means used and the consequences of that treatment than on value judgments about the worth of a particular type of life. Everyone has an equal right to life and we cannot let that right to life "be subject to an intolerable arbitrariness or mere professional inituition."[18] The extraordinary means criterion does not provide specific or detailed rules that can be easily applied, but it does focus on somewhat objective factors and helps to avoid the obvious pitfalls of a policy based upon "a highly discriminatory standard of the worth of a human life,"[19] which is the quality-of-life ethic. It is much more just to make a decision about sustaining life on the basis of the probable outcome of a particular type of treatment than on the basis of the probable outcome of a person's life.

Even when the decision is made, and rightfully made, that a child's life should not be prolonged further, it is not proper to kill. Direct killing of the innocent, even when death is no longer being opposed, "is a blatant violation of the inner worth and dignity of the human person."[20] The parents' right to make decisions regarding the welfare of their child must not be understood to mean that they can do anything they want with that child. A child is not a form of private property; he or she is a unique individual with certain inalienable rights.

Thus Reich argues for the same moral approach to the handicapped infant question that many have used in trying to establish moral policy regarding euthanasia for adults. He does acknowledge, though, some differences that have to be taken into account. In the first place, the infants in question are not all dying; nor can they all be exactly compared to adults who have already lived a full life. "There should be a general presumption that pediatric patients have a higher moral claim on 'extraordinary' medical care than do adults or elderly patients."[21] The fact that a child is abnormal does not mean that he has less claim upon care; rather, the fact that he is a child means that he has more claim. Another difference between the adult and the child is that the child cannot have given consent to the procedure nor has there been any opportunity to get a prior understanding of his personal preferences. "I would take the position that the agent deciding on the child's behalf has the right to make a similar but not identical decision to the one he might make on his own behalf if he were dying."[22] In addition, it is difficult to determine what constitutes extraordinary means in the cases of abnormal infants. The most frequent interpretation of extraordinary means is that it is treatment that has little hope for success. But what is "success" with these infants? "The answer cannot come from medicine alone for it requires a value judgment on the 'quality of life' of a newborn, the foreseen consequences of whose treatment can only partly be anticipated with accuracy at the present time."[23] It is more difficult to determine likely success in an infant than in an adult.

The final representative ethicist is Richard McCormick. In an important essay published in 1974, he takes up, in a sense, where Reich left off. What McCormick is attempting to do in this particular article is to work out the implications of the extraordinary means tradition or, as it was discussed in the previous paragraph, the implications of what it means to say that a treatment will not be "successful."

McCormick suggests that we may be able to arrive at a general guideline to help individuals make appropriate decisions regarding the treatment of handicapped infants.

The guideline is the potential for human relationships associated with the infant's condition. If that potential is simply nonexistent or would be utterly submerged and undeveloped

in the mere struggle to survive, that life has achieved its potential. There are those who will want to continue to say that
some terribly deformed infants may be allowed to die *because*
no extraordinary means need be used. Fair enough. But they
should realize that the term "extraordinary" has been so rela-
tivized to the condition of the patient that it is this condition
that is decisive. The means is extraordinary because the infant's condition is extraordinary. And if that is so, we must
face this fact head-on—and discover the substantive standard
that allows us to say this of some infants, but not of others.[24]

The standard that McCormick is proposing is clear: when a
child, even with treatment, will never have the potential for
human relationships, it is appropriate to withhold treatment and
let him die. Not only is McCormick arguing that it is proper to
decide for death on the basis of the condition or quality of the
child's life, but he is also suggesting that this kind of decision-
making is implied by the traditional distinction between ordinary and extraordinary means itself. While many who reject a
"quality of life" approach to the handicapped infant question
propose instead a focus on means, McCormick suggests that the
traditional focus on means implies a quality of life orientation.

The traditional position has been that there are times when,
even though treatment could be successful in prolonging life, it
is not morally obligatory to treat. As McCormick understands
this tradition, this position was arrived at in defense of the
Christian understanding that all life has a spiritual purpose and
that care for physical life has to be subordinated to concern for
the spiritual. McCormick quotes Pope Pius XII as saying that
an obligation to use every possible means "would be too burdensome for most men and would render the attainment of the
higher, more important good too difficult."[25] When seen in this
light, McCormick argues, it can be realized that certain treatment may be refused because it would lead to a life that does
not have the right quality, a life where things are out of the
proper perspective.

In all these instances—instances where the life could be saved

—the discussion is couched in terms of the means necessary to preserve life. But often enough it is the kind of, the quality of the life thus saved (painful, poverty-stricken and deprived, oppressive) that establishes the means as extraordinary. *That* type of life would be an excessive hardship for the individual. It would distort and jeopardize his grasp on the overall meaning of life. . . . Something other than the "higher, more important good" would occupy first place. Life, the condition of other values and achievements, would usurp the place of these and become itself the ultimate value. When that happens, the value of human life has been distorted out of context.[26]

A careful analysis would reveal, then, that it is the person's condition itself which makes it appropriate at times to discontinue treatment or refrain from treatment. It makes no sense to pursue life when the basic purpose of life cannot be achieved because of the condition of that life. Life itself must be subordinated to other values and is "to be preserved precisely as a condition for other values, and therefore insofar as these other values remain attainable."[27] And "since these other values cluster around and are rooted in human relationships, it seems to follow that life is a value to be preserved only insofar as it contains some potentiality for human relationships."[28]

It is, of course, still going to be a difficult decision. There is no sure way of determining which infants are so abnormal as to be incapable of human relationships. Physicians can and should try to develop ways of attaching relational potential to biological symptoms, ways of determining which symptoms give good reason to think that the child has no potential for human relationships. At this point, we can probably say that the anencephalic infant is without relational potential while the same cannot be said of the mongoloid child.

This is McCormick's proposed guideline for making the decision regarding which infants to treat. Naturally, as with any general guideline, some mistakes will be made. "Risk of error means only that we must proceed with great humility, caution, and tentativeness. Concretely, it means that if err we must at times, it is better to err on the side of life— and therefore to tilt in that direction."[29]

Finally, McCormick argues that his proposal, though the guideline is based on quality of life considerations, does not imply what is sometimes argued under the quality of life concept—that some lives are valuable while others are not. Everyone, regardless of age or condition, is valuable. The point is not that. The point is "whether this undoubted value has any potential at all, in continuing physical survival, for attaining a share, even if reduced, in the 'higher, more important good.' "[30] The individual is valued. The question is whether his life offers any hope of achieving those values for which physical life is the fundamental condition.

Richard McCormick is, in a sense, trying to bridge the gap between those who say the decision should be made on the basis of the means used and not on the basis of the quality of life of the infant and those who say that some lives are not worth living. He sees the extraordinary means approach itself as indicating that it is the condition of life that is decisive. Where the condition of life makes impossible the attainment of the values for which physical life is the condition, there is no reason to preserve that life. This is a quality of life judgment, but is to be made on the basis of biological capacity for relationships, not on any arbitrary judgment about the value of someone else's life.

These, then, are the positions that are being advocated by some of the leading thinkers in the field of medical ethics in the United States today. They do not agree on the best manner of resolving the dilemma, that is clear. They represent views, though, that have to be taken into account by anyone trying to sort out the issues and propose guidelines.

There are at least three key issues on which these ethicists differ. One is the question of whether those who are severely limited in their potential for rationality should be described as non-human, who can claim no right to life or treatment whatsoever. Of the four ethicists just considered, only Fletcher resolves the problem by insisting that we are not dealing with human persons. This would seem to be a most fundamental question: What are we dealing with?

Another dimension of the debate among the ethicists has to do with the basis on which a decision to treat or not should be made. Is it to be made on the basis of the *condition* of the infant? Fletcher and McCormick, though they differ very widely, both answer yes. Smith cannot agree to a decision on the basis of condition and Reich wants to base the decision on the nature of the means being used and its consequences (whether Reich would measure the success of the means in terms of the condition or quality of the infant's life is not clear). Can there really be, as Smith and Fletcher and McCormick all seem to think, no middle ground between treating everyone and deciding which to treat on the basis of quality? In taking a stand on these questions, a hard look will have to be taken at all the implications of a quality of life approach.

The third area of disagreement, which is found here as well as in the larger euthanasia question, is whether letting die is morally different from killing. Smith and Fletcher see no significant moral difference between the two. Reich and, probably, McCormick see a major difference. This is a question that must be answered also before any sort of satisfactory moral understanding of the handicapped infant situation can be arrived at.

# 4
# The Value of Life

In the first three chapters, we have seen the question, examined the context, and listened to some of the proposed answers. Though some interpretation necessarily was involved in the selection of spokesmen and in the analysis of the context, the entire effort was to present an accurate picture of the question and its ethical significance. The remainder of this study is different. It is now time for the author to propose the moral policy which he thinks is most likely, given the context, to contribute to our growth as a just society and as a morally sensitive humanitarian people.

The two parts of the book are not entirely separate, of course; they are the two parts that are necessary to make up the whole. A moral position cannot be wisely taken and defended without a clear understanding of the moral climate of the society. And an argument for one moral approach is most useful when it attempts to show its advantages over alternative approaches. Much of what follows, then, will involve critical reflection on what has been described in the first three chapters.

The preceding chapters have indicated where our emphasis has to be placed. At the forefront is the question of the value of human life, particularly the value of the life of the child born with very different potential, the severely handicapped child. There can be no doubt that much of our attention must be given to the establishment and defense of a position on how to show proper respect for the value of that life.

How does one determine what is morally right or wrong? What makes one course of action right and another wrong? My answer to these questions, the answer I have in mind as I make my criticisms and suggestions, is this: Something is morally right if it produces or is likely to produce beneficial consequences for mankind. What exactly is meant by that simple and somewhat vague statement will become clearer as a position is taken, but a few comments can be made here. The term "beneficial consequences" refers not only to the immediate consequences, but also to long-range ones; it refers to attitudes that may result from practices as well as the consequences of certain actions themselves. Something has "beneficial consequences for mankind" if it contributes to living together in justice and peace and dignity and respect; something is *not* beneficial if it contributes to attitudes and acts of injustice toward one another or involves some form of violation of another. At times, no course of action is open to us that does not involve some injustice or some danger of contributing to injustice in the future. In those cases, what is the right thing to do is that which, among the alternatives, is most in tune with the ideals of justice and peace and dignity and respect.

As regards the question of how best to handle the cases of severely handicapped infants, the right answer is that policy which, in this individual case as well as in the long range, best represents and contributes to justice and human dignity. Both the individual situation and the consequences that are likely to result if a practice becomes widespread need to be considered. There are probably very few cases, if any, which are truly isolated in the sense of not affecting or influencing others. Certainly a policy or guideline should not be proposed without awareness of the impact this might have on the values and attitudes of the general public.

## Human Life

As we have seen, one of the proposed solutions to the problem of how to care for handicapped infants is to propose criteria for humanhood. We should recognize, it has been argued, that a certain capacity for self-awareness and rationality are essential to humanness and that some unfortunate infants do not have this capacity. As a result, they do not need to be treated as human; to bring about the death of one of these infants is in no way a violation of a human good. We might begin to establish our own position by responding to this suggestion.

There are problems associated with Fletcher's proposal, problems so serious that I find it necessary to reject his suggestion. In the first place, we need to think a bit about the implications of *our* deciding that others, because they do not meet certain standards that *we* consider essential for humanness, are not to be treated equally with the rest of us. We are denying others the most fundamental of human rights, the right to life itself. Defenders of social justice have long argued that the only way we can achieve that justice is to recognize that everyone is equal regardless of condition or race or religion or nationality or anything else. What gives a person rights and what makes him worthy of our respect is the simple fact that he is a member of the human race. We cannot establish any other criteria before we recognize fundamental rights. Such rights are inalienable. If we begin to say that the severely retarded infant does not have any human rights, what are we opening the door to in terms of discrimination and injustice?

It is understandable that one might want to say that someone is not human if his capacity for rationality is severely limited or absent. Such a position would provide a standard for making decisions about handicapped infants and would also attempt to clarify, philosophically, the essential difference between men and other animals. Yet, I think there are many reasons to conclude that, understandable though such a proposal might be, it is unacceptable. It is unacceptable because it denies the value of someone else's life on the basis of very questionable, highly speculative, and profoundly dangerous criteria. It destroys life and weakens respect for life without sufficient justification. There are good reasons, I think, for objecting to a definition of humanhood which defines man in terms of the precise difference between him and other animals. That is a little like defining a man or a woman on the basis of the differences between the sexes. Surely what a man and a woman are in common is more fundamental and more important than the differences. What man is in common with other animals may also be of great importance to his very being. It is not so clear that being "self-aware, consciously related to others, capable of rationality" is what it means to say that one is human. I do not propose here, however, to pursue this discussion of the definition of man. Instead, we will look more carefully at the likely social and moral consequences of declaring some not human because of severely limited mental potential.

Social discrimination and the deprival of fundamental human rights because of differences have long been part of human society. Among the most common and most deadly types of discrimination have been those campaigns of hate based upon differences in race or ideology. The centuries of the enslavement of Africans and the centuries of persecutions of the Jews culminating in the holocaust of the Nazis are two outstanding examples of what discrimination can lead to or support. It is hard to think of greater evils and it takes little argument to show that anything contributing directly toward such actions is immoral, unless all alternatives are worse. Discrimination of much less intensity is also a serious evil. The idea that some are more worthy of respect than others, that different persons should be treated unequally precisely because of their differences, must be constantly rejected if we want to avoid some of the great evils that we are always capable of in our treatment of our fellowmen.

To declare some not human because of limited capability is to initiate a policy of discrimination based upon *our* judgment of what is important in human life. We would be setting certain standards and declaring any who do not meet those standards to be without rights. Is this very different from the treatment of Africans or Jews? We would be condemning others to death because they lack what we think is important. What if we realized that mongoloid children could perform very well certain menial tasks that needed to be done? If they are not human, why not use them to labor like slaves or animals? Maybe they could also be used as laboratory research animals. I do not know of anyone who is proposing either of these uses of retarded children, but mentioning them here makes it perfectly clear what is involved in declaring someone non-human. It is well established in our culture that whatever is not human is for the benefit of humankind. If we declare certain infants not human, we may then do with them what we will.

One of the difficulties related to the policy of calling some members of the species not human is the likelihood of beginning to think of some of the rest of us as *more human* than others. If the capacity for rationality is a criterion of humanness, might there not be a tendency to think of those who exhibit minimal rationality as less human than others? It seems that any sort of criteria which excludes some members of the biological species from human rights would almost inevitably result in discrimination among the rest on the basis of who is "more human" or "less human." And such discriminatory attitudes would almost certainly be reflected in our social practices.

We might be willing to chance some of the dangers involved in the practice of declaring some members of the species non-human if we could be fully confident that our criteria were sound. But how do we know that self-awareness or some such capacity is of the essence of humanhood? And how do we know that such and such a child does not have that capacity? There seems to be no indication that widespread agreement on certain criteria for humanhood will be reached soon. Whatever criteria were established would be open to the possibility of being changed or, perhaps, added to as our understanding of what it means to be human changes. As one way of determining humanness, Fletcher proposes that a child be given an I.Q. test and suggests that a minimum score of 20-40 must be achieved before the child can be considered human.[1] How do we know that that is where to draw the line, and on what basis can we object if some begin to suggest that a score of 60 or more is essential?

There are a number of reasons, then, for rejecting the declaration of some infants as non-human as a way of resolving the handicapped infant dilemma. There are practical difficulties as to its workability. There are moral difficulties in denying rights to some members of the species. There are difficulties associated with its possible impact upon our respect for others, especially those who are different or less gifted. For these reasons, I find it necessary to look for other, less dramatic, solutions. Though it may not be possible to prove that these severely handicapped children are human persons, I think it would be totally irresponsible to assume anything else.

To say that these children are all human does not, of course, answer the question about how they should be cared for. But it does eliminate one answer as unacceptable, that which says that these children have no human rights and that their lives are of no value whatsoever. We turn now to another proposed solution.

## Quality of Life

We might look next at the proposal that decisions of this sort ought to be made on the basis of the quality of life of the child. How should we respond to the suggestion that some children may be permitted to die precisely because their conditions are such that their lives will never have much meaning or value? That the decision to treat or not to treat should be made precisely as a judgment about the value of the probable future life of that child? I would respond very cautiously to such proposals and take a close look at as many implications as we can.

There is, of course, always need for a focus on the quality of life, a reminder that how life is lived is of extreme importance. Our focus here on moral values and our concern for the implications of a policy on the way people treat one another are precisely a concentration on the quality of life. But the ethic that uses the term "quality of life" as its trademark makes a specific point. As was noted earlier, it takes the position that some lives are of more value than others because of the condition or meaning of those lives. As Fletcher puts it, life is not good simply because it is human life. It all depends upon the circumstances. If, because of quality considerations, it is not good, then it should not be protected or preserved. It is of the essence of the quality of life approach that not all lives are equally good or equally deserving of protection. The focus cannot be put upon the mere fact of life itself.

The primary advantage of the quality of life approach is that it reminds us that we need to remember that our moral obligations extend further than to the questions of life and death, that we need to be concerned as well with how people live. But what about the way this ethic proposes that we solve questions of life and death? What are the implications for society, for the possibilities of justice and dignity (that is, for the quality of life), of an approach that those who have less potential be treated differently from those who have more potential?

Though she was talking about abortion of deformed fetuses rather than the death of deformed newborns, I think Karen Labacqz's judgment should be carefully considered: "In the long run, this violation of fundamental rights of equal treatment is a more serious threat to the 'quality of life' of all of us than the birth of numerous children with defects will ever be."[2] It is probably true that inherent in the quality-of-life claim that all are not equal in value or have an equal right to protection is the basis for discrimination and injustice that will probably return to haunt all of us and affect, adversely, the quality of all our lives. Many of the dangers associated with declaring retarded infants non-human are also associated with a policy based on judgments about quality.

The decision not to treat certain infants because they will never be capable of "meaningful humanhood" or because they will always be severely retarded or because they can expect a life of suffering or because the parents do not feel capable of caring for a seriously abnormal child is a decision based upon a quality of life judgment. It is a decision usually made in the interest of the child (of that there can be little doubt), and it is a decision with which we sympathize a great deal because of the real severity of many congenital diseases. Nevertheless, there is sufficient reason to refrain from advocating that the decision regarding treatment of handicapped infants should be based upon a judgment on the value of the child's life. The cost may be simply too high.

A primary difficulty is that such a decision involves judging for another that his life is not worth preserving. A judgment not to treat because a life is considered meaningless or of poor quality might be more acceptable if the one whose life is at stake has a voice in such a decision. In the case of the infant, he does not. We are deciding that some weak and defenseless child should not be treated because his life is not of sufficient quality. It has often been said (and I think rightfully) that the moral strength of a people can be measured by the way they treat the weak and defenseless. The practice of letting some of the weak and defenseless die because we don't think that their lives are worth preserving could be an indication of a moral weakness that may affect the lives of all of us.

The decision not to treat on the basis of the probable outcome of the child's life might be seen as an act of discrimination. In the case of the baby with Down's syndrome and duodenal atresia, the decision not to operate was made because the child was a mongoloid child. There is no doubt that if the child was otherwise normal but needed an operation to take care of the intestinal problem, the operation would have taken place and the child would not have been permitted to die. The child was not treated precisely because he was a mongoloid and thus some form of discrimination was involved; less effort was made to preserve the life of that child because of a difference for which the child himself was not responsible.

Can we accept this form of discrimination without contributing to the growth in our society of a policy of treating unequals unequally? I am not so sure we can. Nor am I sure we can decide that someone else's life is not worth being lived without a serious breakdown in our respect for others. The problem with a policy that says life itself is not good but that the goodness depends upon the circumstances is that all the emphasis is placed upon the circumstances. What differentiates one person from another (his unique condition and circumstances) receives more attention than what people are or have in common. It is hard to see how emphasis on circumstances can lead to anything but discrimination and injustice. The fight against discrimination has been made by insisting that, once you get beyond the individual differences, we are all equally good. The quality of life ethic says that once we get beyond the circumstances there is nothing of value whatsoever. The denial of any inherent goodness in human life invites less respect for life.

Sometimes people point to the policies that were in effect in Germany during the time of Adolf Hitler and the Nazi Party as an example of what can happen if the value of individual lives becomes totally subordinated to something else. The suggestion that we are becoming like Nazi Germany is often merely a propaganda statement, one that makes no careful analysis of the differences in conditions and ideology between contemporary America and Germany of a generation ago. On the other hand, the Nazi example is one that should not be ignored. It is one very important example of what could happen to a modern twentieth-century society that accepts official policies that deny the inherent value of each human life and that adopts, as well, an official policy of discrimination. We are not the same as Nazi Germany, but that example may make us even more reluctant to accept a proposal which says that life is not good in itself and that some lives are of greater value than others. We are not Nazi Germany, but it would be most arrogant of any society to think that abuses and extremes can always be avoided and that "it couldn't happen here." The only way to make sure that it doesn't happen here is to be very careful about each new policy that is initiated.

It seems to me that we should proceed, then, toward a decision-making policy in regard to treatment of handicapped infants that is based on the conviction or the assumption not only that these infants are human but also that their lives are inherently good and that they have the very same human rights as more healthy persons. Any other basis is simply not adequate as a protection of the quality of life of all of us.

Though Richard McCormick argues, as was seen in the previous chapter, that it is legitimate to make the decision to treat on the basis of the condition of the infant and though he says that we have to use quality of life language to describe the basis for the decision, he does not advocate the same quality of life approach that has just been criticized. He sees each life as valuable, regardless of condition. Though life itself is good, it is itself merely a condition for a higher good, human relationship. When there is no potentiality for achieving the higher good, then there is no reason to preserve life. Obviously, McCormick's quality of life position is considerably different from the position that I have been arguing is unacceptable and it will be necessary to comment specifically on his ideas.

The question that has to be asked of McCormick's position is whether it has any of the same implications for relative and comparative and unequal valuing of one another. Can one really use a condition of life criterion and still insist that every life is of equal value regardless of condition? I do not ask whether one statement contradicts the other. I think not. But does one statement cancel out the other in the actual ethical climate in which today's debate is taking place? Once McCormick has made the claim that we must decide to treat or not on the basis of the child's condition, will people really be able to pay much attention to his insistence that every life is valuable regardless of condition? How valuable is life anyway if it is only a condition for something else and need not be preserved if that something else cannot be achieved? And though he wants to base his decision on symptoms which physicians can relate to potential for human relationships, is it nevertheless likely that his use of quality of life language will lead others to move away from objective indications to value judgments on the worth of mentally retarded life? These questions are very hard to answer. McCormick's position is itself cautiously stated and his real concern for the handicapped and his moral sensitivity to issues of justice and equality show through. But has he miscalculated the impact of his arguments? Is he, perhaps, guilty of choosing the wrong opponent?

McCormick was apparently led to the acceptance of a quality of life stand out of the conviction that that is precisely the implication of the extraordinary means tradition and that the only alternative is to do everything possible to prolong life. Before I comment further on McCormick's position, I would like to make some observations on the sanctity of life approach and its distinction between ordinary and extraordinary means.

*Sanctity of Life*

The sanctity of life ethic, as the reader will recall, insists that each human life is inherently good regardless of condition and that all lives are of equal value. There is no justification for discrimination based on quality or condition of life and no justification for killing, unless a person has forfeited his right to life by certain actions which are themselves a destruction of or a threat to life itself. On the question of the care of the suffering and dying, this tradition has insisted that it is always a violation of the goodness of life to kill the patient directly or to withhold ordinary means of preserving life. Of the ethicists whose positions were looked at in the previous chapter, Warren Reich is most clearly a spokesman for this ethic.

Without necessarily espousing all the applications that have been made within the tradition, I am convinced that the sanctity of life approach is most useful in forming the attitudes and in inspiring the actions that lead to peace and justice and dignity and respect. By insisting that each person's life is good regardless of condition, it lays the basis for respect for all and for equal treatment for all. By demanding that life be respected as sacred, it emphasizes the limits to the control that man may exercise over life. The right to life, the right to be respected, and the right to equal treatment are all inalienable; they cannot be given or taken away by men. We are constantly made aware by the tradition of our obligation to respect these rights.

In developing guidelines to help people make decisions about how best to care for suffering and dying persons, the sanctity of life tradition has taken two important stands. The first is that letting someone die should not always be considered the moral equivalent of killing, even though death could perhaps be prevented. We will have more to say about this distinction later. The second stand taken is that the way to determine when it is legitimate to withhold treatment is by determining whether the means necessary to preserve life is extraordinary or not. Though it is sometimes acceptable to withhold treatment, such a decision should not be made as a judgment that this life is not good or worthwhile or meaningful any more. Rather, the decision should be one that says that the treatment that would be used to preserve life is destructive of other important goods or not likely to be successful. The key question is whether the means is ordinary or extraordinary.

McCormick has suggested that the talk about extraordinary means is often a hidden way of deciding on the basis of the patient's condition. Often, it is true, there seems to be no clear difference between the two; a means may be extraordinary because of the type of life that would be lived as a result of treatment or continued treatment. Yet many people who use an extraordinary means judgment abhor a quality of life judgment. It seems to me that they see the extraordinary means approach as much more protective of the value of life and of the equality of lives and of decision-making based on somewhat objective criteria. But does it do these things? Is an extraordinary means decision really more protective of the value of life than a decision based explicitly on the condition of the patient?

It would seem to me that the answer to these questions is yes, though perhaps not a resounding yes. By and large, placing the focus on the treatment and its consequences is better than focusing on the quality of life. To decide on the basis of quality is, at the very minimum, to risk the danger of saying that one person is more valuable than another because of his condition. To decide on the basis of means is to be aware of our obligations to care for life and to try to determine the limits of those obligations. Even when the decision is made not to treat further, the process of determining that a particular means is extraordinary places that decision within a context that stresses our obligation to preserve life because it is good. Even though McCormick may be correct in saying that an extraordinary means decision is often a decision based on the condition of life, there seems to be a very important difference in context, a difference that makes the one procedure much more acceptable than the other.

Perhaps the real value of the extraordinary means approach is, then, that it puts the whole question in the context of the goodness of life and of our obligation to respect that goodness. As Reich's statement of the position indicates, this approach emphasizes the goodness of life in two very important ways. First, it does not accept actual killing. Even with the best of motives and even at the request of the patient himself, it is always a violation of the goodness of life to directly kill an innocent person. The goodness of life is inherent; no one, not even the person himself, has a right to destroy that life. When dealing with infants who cannot contribute to the decision of whether to treat or not, this emphasis on the inherent goodness prevents parents or others from assuming that "they have full and prior dominion over the life of the newborn."[3] Secondly, the emphasis on the nature and consequences of the means used provides for some protection against an arbitrary decision being made on the basis of a judgment about the worth of a particular type of life. The decision will still be difficult and may still involve judgments about what constitutes successful treatment, but the focus on means is a constant reminder that we should not decide who should live or die on the basis of the worth of someone's life. This is the entire context of an extraordinary means approach and very clearly it is a context that reflects a profound respect for life.

The extraordinary means approach also makes it perfectly clear that our obligations toward the dying are not ended once the decision is made not to try to save that life. We still have the obligation to care for the dying as he is dying. Our obligation to use ordinary means is still present. There is no abandoning of a person because the decision is made to let die. Even the life of the dying person whose death is not being opposed is good. I'm not sure that a quality of life judgment that a particular life is no longer worth preserving provides much incentive for caring for that person as he dies.

It is precisely this sense of our obligation to respect life as good that makes the sanctity of life ethic the most satisfactory foundation for social living. Not only does it not contain the same dangers of discrimination as the quality of life orientation, but the very fact that the emphasis is placed on our *obligations* is also helpful. It seems that to a great extent the language of *rights* has replaced the language of *obligations* in our moral thinking and in our social movements. The two are not separate, of course. If someone has a right, others have the obligation to recognize that right. But to speak almost exclusively of rights is to concentrate, perhaps too much, on what I have coming to *me*. To talk about obligations is to concentrate more on what we owe to others. We need to do both at times, but there is obviously more danger of conflicts and injustice with most people emphasizing their rights. The sense of obligation toward others which the sanctity of life ethic involves contributes toward respect for one another and, thus, to a higher quality of life.

As we go forward in our attempt to find a just solution to the handicapped infant problem, I suggest not only that these infants be considered human and that their lives be held to be inherently good, but also that we try to resolve the problem in the context of the sanctity of life tradition and its concentration on the means necessary to extend life. There is so much of value in this tradition that the extraordinary means approach should not be abandoned unless it is found to be fully inadequate. I am somewhat in disagreement with McCormick not because he suggests that the extraordinary means tradition implies decision-making on the basis of the patient's condition—it is always helpful to try to work out the implications of a policy—but because he wants us to move toward a quality of life language. As he stated in a later essay, "the thrust of my remarks involved a move beyond the language of ordinary-extraordinary means to the quality-of-life judgments so clearly indicated in them."[4] I am not prepared to change from an extraordinary means language to a quality of life language. There is a whole complex of values that is part of the extraordinary means tradition that, as I have just indicated, is precisely the type of value basis that we need for our whole social life. The complex of values that is usually associated with the quality of life language, though not in McCormick's case, is much less satisfactory and probably very dangerous. I do not see how McCormick can move to the quality of life language without giving some support to the very values that he is personally opposed to. I appreciate his intellectual honesty, but do not see that it would be dishonest to continue to use the language of extraordinary means. Keeping in mind the complex of values associated with both, I find it necessary to use the extraordinary means approach. Nothing else conveys the full implications of our obligations resulting from the goodness of life.

We can now begin to work out the actual implications of

the sanctity of life tradition for the treatment of handicapped infants. We might begin by explaining why the goodness of the infant's life does not necessarily mean that we must always attempt to prolong his life. How can we let anyone die if life is always good?

## Letting Die

David Smith's recognition of the goodness of life led him to the conclusion that, for all practical purposes, there is no justification for letting an infant die untreated. One of the reasons for this conclusion was his conviction that there is no significant moral difference between letting die and killing. What justifies letting someone die is only that which justifies killing.

The extraordinary means tradition argues that there are times when letting someone die is acceptable while killing him would not be. There is, at least at times, a major moral difference between the two types of procedures. I find myself in agreement with this contention. Smith's position puts too much emphasis on the role of man in the matter of life. It does not recognize clearly enough that life is not fully man's to control. Let me explain.

To say that life is good and that its value is not man's to give or take or decide upon is to stand before life with an attitude of acceptance rather than one of control. In the terms that were used in an earlier chapter, we can only really say that life is good in and of itself if we view life as a gift rather than as a possession. Life is to be accepted as a good and taken care of, but the end of life should also be accepted when it comes. Since life is good, it is a violation of a good to kill. But not to preserve a good at all costs cannot be considered the same thing as directly destroying a good. The right attitude toward life seems to be expressed in the sanctity of life's threefold guidelines: directly killing an innocent person is a violation of the goodness of life; failure to use ordinary means of preserving life is an attack upon the goodness of life; the decision not to use extraordinary means, even if the patient dies as a result, is acceptable.

Life itself is not the only good and it is not an absolute good. If the means used to prolong life destroy other important values or if they are not likely to be successful, then it may be a mistake to continue to attempt to preserve life. Death, too, can be a good.

The practice of sometimes distinguishing between directly killing someone and letting someone die by calling the actions "active" and "passive" euthanasia is an unfortunate one. It is unfortunate because letting someone die is never acceptable simply because it is passive, simply because it is not a direct action. It is acceptable, when it is, because it does not constitute an attack upon life at the same time that it recognizes other goods. An omission is not better than a commission, but letting a dying patient go may be compatible with respect for the goodness of life while killing him is not.

Smith has a very good point, though, about the additional difficulty of deciding to let someone die who has not given his consent or whose life is only just beginning. It is true that our obligation to respect the life of the infant has to be interpreted first of all as an obligation to attempt to cure. Nevertheless, even in the case of infants, there can be times when letting die may be compatible with respect for the goodness of that life. It is true, even then, that acceptance of the goodness of life may go hand in hand with the acceptance of death. If death were not inevitable, the two might not go together. But one cannot see the universe as good and to be accepted without seeing death also as something to be accepted. And to accept death means not opposing it at times, just as the acceptance of life as good means not killing.

## Proposed Guidelines

There are several reasons why a study of this sort should include an attempt to draw up some quite specific guidelines on what is morally acceptable and what is not. In the first place, the guidelines force the author to spell out exactly what he means by his general principles; in this case it requires the author to explain exactly how one can emphasize the inherent goodness of all human life while at the same time recognizing the validity of not treating in some circumstances. Guidelines may also be helpful to those who may find themselves called upon to make a decision of this sort. These guidelines will not make their decision easy, but they may provide some ideas that the person will want to keep in mind as he makes the decision. The author's guidelines may also help people to think about the issue carefully, so that they themselves have a good understanding of the type of decision they would make and why. In addition, the attempt to develop guidelines publicly provides others with a chance to respond, to pose alternatives, and, hopefully, to improve our moral awareness and our moral wisdom.

In proposing the guidelines that I do, I am urging persons to use certain criteria for making the decision. If these suggestions are followed, the most important values will be preserved, I am convinced. It is not enough to talk in general about the inherent value of each human life. The actual decisions we make and actions we take must reflect our theoretical values if those values are to survive in any real way.

For reasons that were indicated earlier, I find it most useful to use the language of extraordinary means to establish the extent of our obligation to preserve and extend human life. We need not treat if the means necessary to prolong life are extraordinary. "Extraordinary means of preserving life are all medicines, treatments, and operations which cannot be obtained without excessive expense, pain, or other inconvenience, or which, if used, would not offer a reasonable hope of benefit."[5] Rewording and summarizing the definition, we can say that treatment is extraordinary if (1) it does not offer a reasonable hope of benefit or success or (2) if it imposes an excessive burden. These are the two general categories that will have to be made more specific as regards severely handicapped infants. It is possible, of course, that the burden imposed by a particular treatment may be on the family or on society instead of being a burden on the child himself. The questions that need to be answered, then, are four:

1. What constitutes, in the case of infants, no reasonable hope of benefit or success?

2. When does the treatment of an infant impose an excessive burden on that child?
3. When does the treatment of an infant impose an excessive burden on the family?
4. When does the treatment of an infant impose an excessive burden on society?

The fact that we are dealing with infants definitely affects the answer we give to the question of what constitutes reasonable hope of success. An adult is capable of expressing his own understanding of what would be a successful outcome; a baby is not. An adult may be capable of making the decision himself or of giving his consent; a child is not. For an adult who has long had a grasp on life, success may be interpreted in terms of the fullness of life; for the infant who has never really had much of a grasp on life, just to be alive may be a great success. Both because the infant cannot possibly have a say in the matter and because he is just beginning life, we should use a more minimal sense of success or benefit than we might use for ourselves or other adults. Our obligations toward the weak and the helpless are more stringent than our obligations toward others. We need to be more protective of the most basic goods, like life itself. For a very young infant, any treatment that will probably keep him alive for more than just a few days or weeks should be considered as offering reasonable hope of success. To demand anything more is to deny or ignore the delicate nature of life at that stage.

The first guideline I propose, then, is that any treatment that is likely to keep the child alive for a substantial period of time should be considered as having reasonable hope for success. If such treatment imposes no excessive burdens, we should undertake it at once. If, on the other hand, the child is not likely to survive for a substantial period of time even with treatment, we should not feel an obligation to make the attempt. Such a child, whose death (in all probability) cannot be prevented, is dying. We should care for him as one who is dying and abstain from hopeless efforts or efforts which only prolong the dying. A "substantial period of time" may be several months or one year. I would suggest that if the prognosis is that with treatment the child has a reasonable chance of living a year or more, we should treat that child (provided there are no excessive burdens).

When we are dealing with helpless infants, our obligation to protect and extend life should be rather strictly interpreted. This understanding of what constitutes reasonable hope of success is, I think, such an interpretation. If we are going to go too far in one direction or another, I would prefer that we do so in the direction of protecting the lives of infants. As McCormick has said, "if err we must at times, it is better to err on the side of life."[6] Yet, this interpretation avoids excessive scrupulousness, the obligation to treat even when the case is probably hopeless. Life is a great good and should be protected, but to fight an unreasonable battle against death makes no human sense.

Even though treatment is likely to be successful in the sense defined above, it need not be undertaken if it imposes an excessive burden on the child. But what might such a burden be? Again, I think the benefit of any doubt must be given to preserving life, to deciding that the burden imposed on the child may not be excessive. And, as previously, the fact that we are deciding for an infant who is just beginning life is the reason for wanting to be very slow to decide that a burden is excessive or intolerable. An infant may not be capable of enjoying many of the other values that we know are important in addition to life itself. We should not be quick to decide that some burden is an excessive one for a child to carry so that he may have life itself.

I do not think that the subordination of other values or goods to survival itself is ordinarily an intolerable burden for the infant. But there is a sense in which the burden imposed by life-saving treatment may become excessive. That is when the treatment continues for years. To subordinate everything else to survival temporarily is one thing. To undertake treatment which, even though it is likely to be successful in keeping the child alive, involves a very long, critical battle against death is something else. That kind of treatment may cost too much in terms of the burden imposed, the burden of having to fight continuously for life. Such life-saving treatment imposes a burden on the family as well, but I think it can be considered unnecessary because of the burden it imposes on the child himself. To initiate such treatment is to say to the child that almost all his energy should be devoted for a long period of time to the fight against death. That may be too much to ask of someone. I am not referring, of course, to less burdensome types of treatments that may be life-saving, but to treatments like a long series of critical operations or complete and lengthy dependence on mechanical equipment. Though such treatments may be successful in keeping the child alive, the burden imposed may be tremendous.

We have made it clear that the fact that a child is physically or mentally handicapped should not in itself be considered a reason to withhold treatment and let him die. In spite of these handicaps, his life is good and he should have life-saving treatment. To decide, as was done in the Johns Hopkins mongoloid case, that a child who is mentally retarded should not have a physical condition treated, involves the judgment that someone else's life is not worth living because of his condition. That type of decision-making should not be tolerated in our society. This has been our stance and we remain here. But it is nevertheless true that a very serious mental or physical handicap is a severe burden. If the treatment itself produces this type of a handicap in the process of saving life, the cost might be too high, the burden might be excessive. If, for example, an infant's life can only be saved by brain surgery, which surgery is likely to destroy part of the brain and leave the child severely handicapped, then the treatment might be seen as imposing an excessive burden. In such cases, it would be acceptable to choose not to treat, even though the child dies as a result. To live an entire life severely handicapped is a very heavy burden and, if the treatment itself causes that burden, it may very well be too high a price to pay for life. Life is not an absolute good, to be held onto at all costs.

One can even talk about treatment imposing an excessive burden when it is the timing of a treatment that results in a burdensome life. If, for example, the oxygen supply to the brain has been stopped and the opportunity to resuscitate such a person only comes when it is probable that extensive damage has already been done to the brain, it should be considered an extraordinary means to attempt to restore normal blood circulation, no matter how common the procedure. By saving the life of the patient at this time, an excessive burden would be imposed. McCormick and others would probably say that the decision not to treat in such a case is based on concern for the quality of the life of the child. And, of course, they are largely correct. Yet, I think it is still useful to speak of this as treatment imposing a burden. It is not the child's condition before the immediate situation that warrants the decision not to treat, but the fact that treatment here and now would result in the burden that would have to be carried. He would not have this burden if it were not for this treatment now.

The second guideline, then, is this: treatment imposes an excessive burden on the child himself if it involves a long, drawn-out battle against death or if the treatment itself results in a severe and permanent handicap. Such treatment should be considered extraordinary and may be withheld without violating the child's right to life.

What about excessive burdens that might be placed on the family or on society? Are there any situations where the effect that a certain course of treatment has on the family or society renders that treatment extraordinary? Earlier, in considering the ways in which others are approaching the issue, we noted that some appear to make their decision primarily in terms of the child's own interest and others seem to stress the effect that child's life and treatment have on others. The guidelines just discussed are an attempt to indicate when, in the child's own interest, there is good reason to refrain from treatment. We are now turning to the other question. What justifies not treating the child for the sake of others?

The basic answer must be that we are doing an injustice to the child if we allow him to die because of the burden that he, as a result of his condition or his treatment, is imposing on others. If we want life to be valued as a good and individuals to be considered important in themselves, we cannot tolerate a policy of deciding for death for someone because he is a burden to others.

Even if we are primarily concerned with society and not just with the individual, we should recognize this. All of us will likely suffer in the long run if we begin to think of the right to life of individuals in terms of the ways in which they affect others. The answer to the question of whether we should focus on the child's interests or the interests of society is that we must focus on the individual child, both for his sake and for society's sake.

Yet this general rule does not mean that we should never be concerned with the context in which an individual lives. We are, after all, not just individuals; we are individuals who are part of a whole. We cannot be fully aware of our obligations to others if we always focus on the individual and never on the group in which the individual finds meaning and responsibilities. We need to emphasize that the individual is good and valuable in and of himself; at the same time, we need to recognize that individuals also have obligations to the larger whole. In terms of the question of when is it acceptable to withhold treatment of handicapped infants, this balanced reading of the relationship between the individual and the social unit suggests that it is proper to seek to know what kind of a burden the treatment will place on the family but not proper to worry about the burden imposed on the larger society.

A child is a member of a family in a unique sense. His very identity is as part of the family. Though some dimensions of the family institution may be artificial and arbitrary, the family itself is a natural social unit; one simply cannot come to be without having a mother and a father. It is in the family unit, then, that it is important to recognize that no individual exists alone. On the other hand, the individual is not that directly or intimately a part of the larger society. To begin to decide for or against life for someone on the basis of the burden imposed on society is much less defensible. You are no longer talking about a very tangible burden imposed on a specific individual or specific individuals. It is easy to see the dangers involved in the "burden on society" type of reasoning. This could lead directly to dismissing the inherent value of the individual. A somewhat similar danger exists with the family focus, but it is less serious and can be more easily guarded against.

I would suggest that treatment of a child may be withheld if the treatment imposes an excessive burden on the family. Something can be considered an excessive burden on the family if it very probably prohibits the essential functioning of the family. It is not easy to give examples of cases where the treatment imposes too heavy of a burden on the family. One might think of expense or of extended intensive treatment, but it is most difficult to know when these constitute an excessive burden. The family exists for the members, so that a burden would have to be very intense indeed before it could be considered excessive. It is true that the family unit should not destroy itself in the pursuit of life for one member, but we must be very slow to conclude that such destruction is taking place. While recognizing that not everything should be sacrificed in the saving of the life of one family member, we should guard against the danger of using "burden on the family" as an excuse for neglecting to care for a handicapped child.

The concept of excessive burden on the family is a fair, though difficult, concept to use in trying to decide whether to treat or not. It is important to insist, however, that it is only justifiable not to treat because of this burden when it is the *treatment* that imposes the burden. Any handicapped child, by his very condition, imposes a burden on the family. And that burden can be very heavy. But the burden that the condition of the child imposes on the family is not sufficient reason not to treat, to let the child die. In the family, especially, one should be accepted as good regardless of his condition. The family obligation is to accept and love and take care of the handicapped member and, if necessary, to get aid in doing so. To let someone die because of the burden his condition imposes on the family is to bring a most serious form of injustice right into the family itself. It is the family's obligation to care for a member, or see that he is cared for, regardless of his handicaps.

Yet, the situation is a little different if it is the treatment that imposes a burden on the family. It is one thing to accept a family member regardless of condition and the burden imposed by that condition. It is another thing to deliberately undertake treatment for one member of the family when that treatment itself will impose an extremely heavy burden on other members of the family. Life is a good and is to be preserved, but not at too high of a cost. It is legitimate to recognize the burden to the family as part of the cost to be taken into account.

This third guideline must remain a general one. Life-saving treatment may be withheld if the treatment itself imposes an excessive burden on the family. Such treatment may not be withheld if it is the condition rather than the treatment that imposes the burden. For example, letting a mongoloid die because to raise such a child is very burdensome violates the goodness of life. To choose to let a child die rather than to undertake treatment which means the relocation of the entire family in a different climate without good hope for employment may be compatible with respect for life. The difference between not treating because of the nature of the treatment and not treating because of the nature of the condition may seem a somewhat artificial one. After all, a burden is a burden. But the difference is very real. It is the difference between not bringing about a burden which does not now exist and rejecting a burden that is part of one's familial responsibility. It is proper for a family to decide whether a certain treatment is appropriate and to weigh the consequences of that treatment on the family in making the decision. That follows from the realization that the preservation of life is not an absolute good and from an understanding of familial relationships. But to decide not to treat (when the treatment is not itself burdensome) because the child's condition is burdensome to the family is to reject the fundamental obligation to view all lives as inherently good and equally valuable. It is a little like the difference between choosing to avoid conception because a child would be a burden at this time and rejecting a child who is born because he is a burden. There are times when avoidance of a course of action which would be burdensome is wise; there are times when acceptance of an already existing burden is the only appropriate response.

A practical way of determining whether the decision not to treat a child is being made on the basis of the child's condition or because of the nature of the treatment is to answer truthfully one question: would I treat if the baby would be perfectly normal after treatment? Presuming that the parents love their child and are not simply rejecting him, a "no" answer means that it is the treatment that is burdensome while a "yes" answer means that it is the child's condition that is most important in the decision.

We do not recognize any circumstances where the very treatment of a child would impose an intolerable burden upon society. When many handicapped infants are cared for in state institutions, taxpayers are burdened. But such a burden is not intolerable or excessive. As a society or as a group, we need constantly to care for these unfortunate ones among us. It is true that individuals have a moral obligation not to impose a burden on others, but that is true only when it can be helped. To talk about letting someone die because he imposes a burden on society is to approach the whole question in the wrong way. Individuals do not have their meaning in terms of society or the state, but society and the state have their meaning in terms of individuals. In this century of totalitarian governments, the dangers associated with letting people die because of some notion of a burden to society are so great that the only defensible moral guideline seems to be this: treatment may *not* be withheld because of any burden imposed upon society. I simply cannot understand how treatment that has reasonable hope of success and does not impose an excessive burden on the child or on the family can impose an excessive burden on society.

Let me repeat and summarize the suggested guidelines to be used in making the decision about whether or not to treat a handicapped infant. Every handicapped infant should be treated *unless*:

1. The treatment is not likely to be successful. That is, the child is not expected to live for more than a few months even with the best of treatment.

or

2. The treatment imposes an excessive burden on the child. For example, he can expect a very long period of intensive fighting for life or the treatment itself results in a severe and permanent handicap.

or

3. The treatment imposes an excessive burden on the fami-

ly. Such would be the case if the treatment placed the continued existence of the family as a functioning unit in very serious jeopardy.

It might also be repeated that the above guidelines in no way imply that some, because healthier or more normal, have more right to life than others. If these guidelines are carefully followed, one would be able to avoid showing less respect for the retarded than for the mentally normal, something that is almost impossible to do when decisions are made on the basis of the condition of the child.

### The Moral Climate

The notion of moral climate has surfaced from time to time in this study. One of the underlying presuppositions has been that a moral question and a moral position should always be seen in the larger context, in the context of the moral debate and the moral values present in society. It is for this reason that we examined the moral positions on abortion and euthanasia. It is for this reason that we looked at the various positions being taken on the handicapped infant question. Only by paying close attention to the moral climate can one get a real sensitivity for the full dimensions of a question. Now that the guidelines have been proposed and explained, it is useful to look at the moral context again and to consider the ways in which this position speaks to that context.

Without attempting to explain fully a position on abortion and adult euthanasia, I would like to indicate briefly three ways in which the stand taken here speaks to those questions. It is my hope that certain characteristics of the stand taken here not be ignored by the reader as he or she considers abortion and adult euthanasia.

The first is the emphasis on the goodness of life itself. Perhaps it would be an enriching experience for more persons to think and speak of life as a gift and to reflect upon the implications of gratitude. I'm not so sure that talk about the right of the woman to control her reproduction or the right of the fetus to life or any other right is as valuable to our moral sensitivities as talk about acceptance and gratitude and obligations resulting from the gift of life itself. It seems to me that we may lose some of our ability to find a satisfactory solution to our ethical dilemmas if we do not remind ourselves, now and again, that there is a certain sense of awe that we should have toward life.

A second dimension of the above stand that may relate to the abortion and euthanasia discussions is the emphasis on the social dimensions of the sanctity-of-life approach. The idea seems to have developed among some people that the quality-of-life ethic is more concerned about the conditions under which people live than is the sanctity-of-life ethic. As was indicated above, the sanctity approach is concerned about how the quality of our lives will be affected if we do not respect life as sacred in and of itself. We need to define quality not just in terms of mental and physical health or in terms of a high standard of living or in terms of ability to control one's own life; we also need to realize that conditions of life are affected by the respect that we have for one another. It is probably not too much to say that the attitudes we foster are the most important ingredients in developing a high quality of life.

A third characteristic of the above stand that might be kept in mind in other ethical dilemmas is the willingness to make difficult distinctions and to draw lines. It is not an easy task and usually not an agreeable one, but one that should often be part of our ethical analysis. Whenever there is more than one value at stake (as is almost always the case), we need to try to keep the various values in mind and to do justice to all of them. But that cannot really be done without ranking these values and developing guidelines to show when one might be sacrificed for another. A substitute for that type of line-drawing is to simply urge the individual to keep various things in mind as he decides. But it is much more useful, I would maintain, to suggest how to do that, to suggest which values should outweigh other values in certain cases.

Another value of being willing to draw up guidelines is that it helps to focus attention on *what* is being done. In other words, it is not just a plea for someone to act lovingly or compassionately but a clear indication that what is loving or compassionate depends largely upon what actions are being taken. We must be willing to draw lines if we are going to avoid the pitfall of suggesting that morality is only a matter of intention and motivation. Many, many persons have been terribly harmed by someone who acted with the best of intentions.

In these three ways, at a very minimum, the position taken here on treatment of handicapped infants has much to say to those who are taking positions on related questions. There is another way, as well, in which we might consider the possible role of this position in the development of a moral climate. What does it have to say to those who approach the question of treatment of handicapped infants on the basis of one of the six primary values considered in the previous chapter? How does it support or discourage each of those attitudes? (These are not detailed criticisms but brief indications of the types of critiques that follow from the stand taken here.)

For those who approach the question out of a desire for *the least possible suffering*, the above stand suggests two reminders. The first is that there is a difference between causing suffering and enduring suffering. To cause suffering is something that we should always try to avoid when possible. But to endure suffering is not always evil. Suffering is a little like death: it is terrible to bring it about unnecessarily, but one can often act nobly in accepting it. A second reminder is that while the goal of reducing suffering is an admirable one, the means used to achieve that goal may defeat the purpose. It is possible to pursue that goal in such a way that more, not less, suffering results in the long run. For example, what would happen if we adopted the policy that one person may decide for another whether he is suffering too much to be allowed to live? It is certainly possible that this may lead to saying that there are other conditions as well that make life not worth living. And it does not take much imagination to think that much suffering will be the result in a society in which some judge other lives not worth living.

There is much agreement between our position and that of those whose primary value is *the protection of life*. Both agree on stressing the obligation of parents to protect the lives of their children. But the position taken here acknowledges that not everything need be done to extend lives. Life is not an absolute good and, though an infant should not be directly killed, there are some circumstances when death need not be opposed. Basically, though, our position supports the protection-of-life approach.

There are those who approach this question in terms of *the welfare of society*. The arguments made above suggest that these individuals think again before pursuing that line of decision-making. In the first place, we need to be very careful in determining what constitutes "benefit for society." Practical considerations, questions like financial cost and use of resources, are very important but, in the long run, they may be nowhere as important as the types of attitudes toward life and toward the disadvantaged that we encourage and support. There is a real danger of sacrificing what constitutes real quality living in society for the sake of "practicality." The position that has been taken here also challenges defenders of the welfare-of-society approach to think very carefully about subordinating the welfare of the individual to the welfare of the larger social group. The dangers inherent in this sort of subordination need to be kept constantly in mind.

Though our position recommends the acceptance of the natural as good, it does not agree that we resolve our moral dilemmas by what is sometimes called nature's rule, *the survival of the fittest*. The survival-of-the-fittest ethic tends to put all of the emphasis on the survival of the species and very little on the value of the life of the individual. As was argued above, the subordination of the individual to the race leads to a denial of the inherent value of every human life, something which we cannot permit if we hope to achieve some measure of peace and social justice. There is another difficulty with the survival-of-the-fittest thinking. That is the suggestion that survival itself is always the most important value. I am not so sure that it is. There may be some prices just too high to pay, such as the complete hardening of our hearts to the needs of the disadvantaged. It is not life itself that is the greatest good, even the survival of the race, but the quality of our living. One of the basic characteristics of quality living is respect for the goodness of each individual life.

Though our comments did not, for the most part, respond directly to *the freedom of conscience* school of thought, the whole character of this chapter constitutes a criticism of that approach. We have been offering definite suggestions on how persons should decide on the question of treating handicapped infants while the freedom-of-conscience ethic argues that we should try to refrain from influencing another's decision. A good moral decision demands careful consideration of what is involved and of what the implications of various ways of acting may be. Someone is not helped much toward that kind of wise decision-making by one who simply says that each person should do what he or she thinks is best; he may be helped toward a better understanding by one who takes and defends a position. It is true that it is important not to deny individual freedom of conscience. It is also very important, though, to provide stimulation for serious reflection on moral questions. Urging someone to accept a particular position for certain reasons is not the same as "imposing a position." There is a second difficulty with the freedom-of-conscience ethic. If freedom is the primary value, then *what* one does is not so important. What the ethic demands is simply that we act freely and respect the freedom of others, that each person be free to do whatever he thinks is right. This tendency to deny the importance of what is being done is somewhat qualified by a concern for others, the usual expression being "as long as no one else is hurt." Our discussion has been an attempt to determine precisely what type of policy or action *is* likely to hurt others. It is the implication of the freedom-of-conscience ethic that these decisions will not hurt others while this study strongly suggests that the way in which people go about deciding these life and death questions is almost certainly going to affect others. The freedom ethic underestimates the extent to which our thinking and acting affect others, for good or for harm.

The final view that was discussed in the previous chapter is the view of those who place the emphasis on *sufficient mental capacity*. This kind of thinking has been directly responded to in the above arguments. It is true that physical life is not the fullest meaning of human life, but we must keep in mind the implications of deciding who should live and who should not on the basis of the fullness of life. Such decisions open the door widely to discrimination and injustice.

The position taken and the guidelines proposed in this chapter have been arrived at with every attempt to understand the context and the possible impact of a proposal upon the moral climate. The validity of a position depends largely upon whether or not it provides the kind of values needed in today's moral climate.

# 5
# Making the Decision

There are, it would seem, three necessary parts to a thorough ethical study of the deformed infant question. The first is to analyze the various values involved, explore the context, and suggest guidelines that ought to be followed. This is the primary task and the one that has engaged us up to now. The second is to reflect upon the actual decision-making process and, with a view to safeguarding the most important values, to comment upon the proper roles of the individuals involved. That will be done in this chapter. The third task is to consider the obligations of the larger public in the issue and to suggest a legal policy that reflects those obligations. This will be the work of the final chapter.

The first question that must be answered in this chapter is the question of who should decide. Who has the primary responsibility to make the decision about whether or not to treat a severely handicapped infant? The second question is just as important. What are the obligations of all the parties involved to ensure that the decision is made with full awareness of the implications? It is the second question that will receive most of our attention here. It is so important that the one who has to decide give himself and be given by others full opportunity to make a wise decision.

## Who Should Decide?

Since the very young child is not himself capable of making the decision about treatment, someone has to make the decision on his behalf. There are perhaps five candidates for the position.

First, the child's parents or guardian. Second, the physician or the medical staff. Third, a judge or someone else acting as a representative of the larger society. Fourth, a moral counselor or a clergyman. Fifth, a committee made up of some or all of the above.

It is our judgment that the parents have the greatest claim to the authority to make a life and death decision of this sort. As was argued in the previous chapter, a child is a member of a family in a more complete sense than he is a member of any other group. There is, as well, a very great likelihood that the parents will have the child's own real interest at heart. Parents have the primary responsibility in the raising of their children and they must be recognized as having the primary responsibility of making the decision of whether or not to treat a severely handicapped infant.

The physician, though he has a very important part to play, should ordinarily not be the one to make the actual decision. Such a decision is an ethical decision, not precisely a medical one. While it can only be made wisely when there is sound medical information, the decision itself is largely one of values. We should not ask physicians to make moral decisions for others.

In the previous chapter we rejected the idea of letting a child die for the sake of society; so, too, should we reject the idea of letting some representative of the larger society make the decision for the family about who should live and who should die. There is one sense, though, in which this should probably be done. Society has an obligation to protect the innocent from harm, even from harm at the hands of family members or parents. It is probably necessary to have and enforce laws which restrict somewhat the freedom of parents to choose death for their children. But society's role is to set the limits of what can be permitted; it is not to make the ordinary decisions for the parents.

The suggestion that a moral counselor be the one to make the decision has the advantage of recognizing the moral nature of such a decision, but all of us need to make our own moral decisions, not have an "expert" make them for us. Such a moral counselor may have, like the physician, an important role to play but that role does not include making the actual decision.

The idea of a decision by a committee should also be rejected. It is a way of recognizing that the decision is not totally an individual one, but it is likely to unnecessarily restrict the role of parents in their own families. For the same reasons that we do not want a physician or a judge or a moral counselor to be the one who makes the decision, we do not want a committee made up of these to do so.

The decision should be made by the parents. There is no one else who is as close; there is no one else who would have as much involved in treatment; there is no one else who is as likely to have to live with the consequences of the decision; there is no one else who has the same daily responsibility toward the child.

This does not mean, of course, that parents can do whatever they want with their own children. They do not own them. All of us must guard against the abuse of parental authority in the care of handicapped children (the role of the law in this regard will be discussed in the next chapter). In making their decision, parents need to get information and advice. Others need to provide that information and advice. Let us reflect on the full responsibilities of those involved—the medical staff, the moral counselor, the parents themselves.

### The Medical Staff

It is obvious that the very first responsibility that medical personnel have when the question arises about whether or not to treat a severely handicapped infant is to inform the parents as to the exact nature of the child's condition, the nature of the treatment, and the probable outcome with treatment and without treatment. (Perhaps this should be called the second responsibility, the first being the accuracy of the diagnosis itself. But that, I am sure, goes without saying.) It may be very difficult for parents to grasp the true nature of their child's condition and of the nature of the possible treatment, already overwhelmed as they are likely to be by the tragedy of the abnormality. It is essential that every effort be made to explain things in ways that the parents will understand.

It is also important that the physician and the staff understand that the decision to be made is a moral one, not precisely a medical one. This fact has several implications.

In the first place, it needs to be made clear that the decision is the parents' to make, that the doctor will not make it for them. Parents should be encouraged to get help as they make the decision; it should be recommended that they get some moral counseling or moral advice. This does not mean a long series of consultations, but simply an opportunity to discuss the question with someone who is well acquainted with the moral implications. Naturally the parents should be encouraged to see whomever they have confidence in as a moral counselor, but the hospital should also be able to recommend qualified persons who can help the parents in this way. In light of the ethical questions related to modern medicine, it is important that every hospital be able to recommend someone as moral counselor for patients and the families of patients. It is important that parents be strongly urged to get advice on whether to treat their abnormal child. Just as they cannot wisely make the decision without medical information so they cannot expect to be acting wisely without an understanding of the moral implications. It is not the medical staff's responsibility to explain those implications, but it is their responsibility to suggest moral counseling and, perhaps, to find a moral counselor for them.

The distinction being made here between medical and moral raises a very important question about the moral role of medical personnel. Should members of the medical staff themselves engage in moral counseling? Certainly many of them have given much consideration to the propriety of non-treatment in cases of severely handicapped infants. What are their responsibilities in this regard?

There is a danger, sometimes, of what might be called a "confusion of expertise." This occurs when someone who is competent in one area is automatically presumed to be competent in another, unrelated, area. It happens especially when someone is a member of a well-respected profession, such as medicine. The great progress that medicine has made in many areas has led some people to think that those who work in medical science are endowed with competence which far exceeds the strict confines of that science. In terms of our concern here, there are some who may give a physician great moral authority simply because he is a physician.

If physicians act as moral counselors, this confusion of expertise may be the result. If they suggest or recommend a particular decision, the recommendation might be taken, by some, as "doctor's orders." It is important that this not happen. The parents need to recognize that the decision is theirs to make and that they have to assume responsibility. The parents, and all the rest of us, need to remember that these are moral decisions, not medical ones. Unless that is clearly understood, there is no chance of being fully aware of the implications.

Because this possibility exists that the physician's moral advice will not be taken for what it is, it may be best for him to refrain from giving advice on the question. He should, of course, use his judgment. Where it is evident that the parents will take the physician's expression of his moral point of view as the conviction of a private individual and not as a statement carrying the authority of medical science, then such a conversation would be very proper and probably quite helpful. But this is often not the case; the better general rule may be to refrain from giving advice. Such a rule should not be taken to mean that physicians should not have strong moral views or that it is unprofessional to express them. It is merely a way of guarding against misunderstanding on the part of the parents.

There is another conclusion that follows from the realization that this is a moral not a medical decision that is being made. All members of the staff must insist upon their responsibility of being true to their own consciences. There is no necessity to go along with the parents' decision if one thinks that it is totally inappropriate or unethical. Every member of the staff needs to know what he will be part of and what he will have to object to on moral grounds. This may, of course, exert some pressure on the parents, but that is as it should be. To say that parents have the primary responsibility in making the decision does not mean that others should abandon their own sensitivities or do everything possible not to influence the decision. Influence very definitely has a place; moral decisions are often best made as one reflects upon and responds to the moral positions of others. The only thing that needs to be guarded against —and this is the basis for the above caution—is the taking of moral advice as a professional medical statement. Where it is perfectly clear that the position is a moral one, as when someone refuses to take part in a certain procedure, there should be no hesitation on the part of the staff to express their moral views.

It is equally proper for a member of the medical staff or for the hospital to use legal means to protect a child from his own parents. There are limits to parents' control over their own children and every citizen should recognize some responsibility to protect children from harm. It is in no way contrary to a professional relationship to the family to request, for example, that law enforcement authorities investigate whether child abuse laws are being violated.

In summary, then, the responsibility of the medical personnel involves giving medical information, encouraging parents to make the decision with the help of moral counseling, taking whatever moral stands they themselves think appropriate, and protecting the child from an abusive decision. All this means that staff members should have carefully considered for themselves the morality of a "let die" practice in the care of severely handicapped infants. It is not theirs to make the primary decision, but it is theirs to consider very carefully what should be done.

If the decision is made to let die and if there is no reason to object to this decision, there is one further responsibility that falls upon the staff. That is the responsibility to continue to care for the dying child as he dies. It is always difficult to care for the dying; it may be most difficult in the case of an infant whose death is, in a sense, chosen. When no attempts are being made to extend the life of the child, respect for life entails care in the sense of trying to make the child as comfortable as possible and of giving the child as much attention and love as possible. The decision not to treat does not in any way justify neglect.

## The Moral Counselor

Many of us seem to be very reluctant to give moral advice. There are several reasons for this. We are aware that there are those who do not really want to assume responsibility for their own decisions and actions; they would definitely prefer that someone decide for them. We hesitate to give advice for fear of encouraging that lack of responsibility. In addition, we are very much aware of the fact that we live in a morally pluralistic society. People do not agree on moral questions. And it seems somewhat arrogant to suggest that one particular position is better than others. Perhaps most important, we value freedom of conscience very highly. We do not in any way want to destroy or diminish another's freedom as he makes his moral decision, and we are somewhat afraid that suggestions on how someone should act may be pressure that reduces his freedom.

On the other hand, we are not always satisfied when we receive moral advice that simply presents the alternatives and asks us to choose the one that makes most sense. Very often what we want to know is which makes more sense in the advisor's opinion. We sometimes like to have persons, especially those whom we respect, tell us what they think we should do. We can then decide with the advantage of their wisdom. This is especially true in questions which are quite complex and which the advisor may have given much more thought to than we have.

Given these different attitudes, what ought the moral counselor do and say as he or she tries to help parents make the difficult decision about treatment for their abnormal child? It is, of course, almost as difficult to make suggestions to the advisors as it is for them to help the parents, but there are some things that can be said about the responsibilities of moral counselors in these cases.

In the first place, it is essential that those who serve as moral counselors on the question of how best to care for the severely handicapped child be very well informed as to the nature of the moral debates that have been taking place. They need to be acquainted with what others have said and to have worked out their own position. One of the primary services they can offer the parents is an informed explanation of the moral implications of various proposed solutions. Just as parents expect the physicians they consult on the child's condition to be well acquainted with that type of a problem, so they should be able to expect that their moral counselor is fully familiar with the moral issues and is clear on where he himself stands.

In the actual discussions with the parents, there is need for the counselor to be very aware of the particular situation and to recognize the particular needs of these individuals. So he must be quite adaptable and cannot follow a set agenda. But it is possible to indicate some of the things that should ordinarily be done.

It is the counselor's responsibility, as I see it, both to present alternative courses of action with the reasons that might suggest each and to give a definite recommendation for a course of action that is, in the counselor's opinion, more defensible than any other. To present the alternatives is to make it clear that the choice is the parents'. It is also a means of discussing some of the advantages and disadvantages that may not have been seen by the parents. In general, a consideration of the options contributes to a more informed decision. To advise a particular course of action is to give the parents the benefit of the counselor's study and convictions. It serves as well as a way of reminding the parents that, though they are the ones who make the decision, no decision, especially a life and death one, is without its impact on others. Thus, the convictions of others should be heard.

The alternatives that are open to the parents and that need to be discussed are more than just to treat or not to treat. They include such possibilities as placing the child in an institution (after treatment or without treatment), taking the child home, beginning treatment with the possibility of discontinuing it later, etc. In the discussion of options, the parents may be able to see much more clearly what exactly their concerns are. Once the parents' primary concerns become clearer, the counselor can discuss the advantages and disadvantages of different courses of action largely in terms of those concerns.

It is not enough, though, to simply present the alternatives and the pros and cons of each. There is a need as well (at least ordinarily) for the counselor to suggest one particular course of action as most protective of the most important values. It is important, of course, that this be done in the right manner. Such advice should not be given in a manner that suggests that the final word has been said. On the other hand, the suggestion should not be made apologetically. The counselor needs to avoid two dangers: he should not manipulate the parents into doing what he suggests against their own best judgment; he should not present his own position so weakly that it seems as though he does not believe in it very deeply.

One of the reasons why the counselor should advocate his own position is that the moral climate of today demands it. We are so aware of the value of freedom and of the danger of "imposing" a moral position on another that we may be losing sight of the importance of *what* we do. If our whole focus is on freedom and tolerance, we come very close to saying that what one does is not so important, as long as it is done freely. We need to balance our concern for freedom with an emphasis on the nature of the action and one of the best ways of doing that is to recommend a particular course of action.

If our stress on freedom and tolerance suggests that it is intolerance to tell someone what we think he should do or that he has done wrong, then we are backing ourselves into a corner. What can we then do or say if, at times, we do as a matter of fact think that someone's behavior is "wrong," as in some criminal activity? Our moral rhetoric would not permit us to say that he or she did wrong. So we might look for another way out, perhaps by saying that the person must be "sick" or that the social conditions caused him to do it. The result is that, in the pursuit of a morality of individual freedom, we may end up denying freedom and responsibility! To preserve real freedom, we need to be most interested in how that freedom is to be used.

The reluctance to recommend a particular course of action

seems to imply that actions and the consequences of actions are not so important when talking about morality, that morality is primarily a matter of internal attitudes and intentions. Intentions and attitudes are, of course, very important in morality; so are actions. Actions themselves have consequences, sometimes quite different from what was intended. If we lose the realization that consequences are important and that the exact nature of the consequences depends much more upon the actions than upon the intentions and attitudes, then we are losing a most important basis for personal and social responsibility. Responsibility for others can only be fostered by an emphasis on *what* is to be done. Nothing else says so clearly that the course of action is important than the recommendation that a particular course of action be chosen. The moral counselor, by advocating a particular course of action, is expressing his own sense of responsibility toward the consequences of that decision.

Moral counseling should not be the same as psychological counseling. A psychological counselor is not so concerned with what a person does as with how he views himself. His goal is that the person be able to understand himself and live with himself and his decisions. Psychologists usually adopt the scientific model, which insists that one should be objective, that his personal values should not enter into his professional work. Psychological counseling, then, usually involves a refusal to talk about what is right or good.

The moral counselor, on the other hand, has a certain loyalty and obligation to the right and the good. His role in this case is not primarily to help the parents be at peace with themselves but to help them make the best decision. He should be very concerned about internal dispositions, but also very concerned about actions and the consequences of actions. His commitment to the good does not permit him to be value-free. It is very much a part of his role to recommend a particular decision.

As was mentioned earlier, it is absolutely essential that the moral counselor exercise his role of advice-giving with discretion. He has to recognize that his view is not the only one, that other thoughtful and compassionate men have reached different conclusions. And he should convey this understanding. The parents, being faced with such a decision, should be given the full benefit of the counselor's study of the moral implications as well as the benefit of the wisdom of the moral tradition in which the counselor has been trained. But such advice should always be presented in a way which permits the parents to disagree. The counselor should recommend a particular decision, but not make that decision for the parents.

Once the decision has been made, the moral counselor should turn his attention to helping the parents prepare for what comes next—whether it be the caring for the handicapped child or the loss of a child. Though he may not agree with their decision, he needs to recognize that the decision was theirs, not his, to make and to give them credit for seeking moral counseling and for making a very difficult decision to the best of their ability.

The role of the moral counselor in the decision-making process can be a very important one. It demands a great deal of preparation; what is especially important is that he or she have studied and reflected deeply on the moral nature of the question. It demands skill as moral advisor; he or she should be able to give advice without deciding for someone else and to listen sympathetically and understandingly without hiding one's own moral convictions. With the help of a good moral counselor, the parents will be able to make the decision with a better understanding of what, in a moral sense, they are choosing and rejecting.

## The Parents

In a real sense, everything that has been said in this study relates to the parents' responsibility in making the decision. They need to be aware of the moral context; they need to examine carefully the moral implications of different solutions; they need to become very clear on the value of infant human life. In addition, they need to get whatever help they can in making the decision, especially all pertinent medical information and the advice of a qualified moral counselor. There are, however, a few additional points that need to be made here about the parents' responsibility.

A decision of this sort is always going to be difficult for the parents to make. Even with the use of guidelines like those suggested in the previous chapter, the right decision is rarely going to be perfectly obvious. Guidelines can be very helpful in the decision-making process, but the application of guidelines is not the same as the application of a mathematical formula or the use of a logical syllogism. The decision remains a decision, open to second thoughts, and not a non-debatable conclusion. The use of particular guidelines may make the final decision much easier, but the choice of those guidelines is itself always going to be debatable. The parents should recognize, then, that the choice is going to be difficult and that they may very well have second thoughts later.

The decision is going to be difficult, but it should not be arbitrary. Since the right or best decision can in no way be demonstrated to everyone's satisfaction, there may be a tendency to think that reasons are not so important, that one might as well choose somewhat arbitrarily. That would be a mistake. Parents should be able to know their reasons and explain them to their own satisfaction. It is only when reasons for and against a certain procedure have been wrestled with that one can really be sure that he has decided carefully. People disagree on what is morally right and, to some extent, it is true to say that what is moral is a matter of opinion, but that does not mean that such an important decision as whether a deformed child should be treated should be an unfounded opinion, made a certain way simply because the parents "feel" that that would be best. Recognizing the need for reasons protects somewhat against arbitrariness and ensures some attention to the issues at stake.

There are some dimensions of the parent-child relationship that need to be kept in mind as parents make their decision. It has been pointed out earlier that children should never be regarded as the property of the parents. Parents do not own children; parents do not have the right to do whatever they want with their children. For our purposes, it is better to speak of the obligations rather than of the rights of parents. They have the obligation to care for their children and the obligation to protect them from harm. They also have the obligation to make decisions that seriously affect the future of their children. In making decisions for a child, parents should remember that a child is a child; it is not always the same as deciding for an adult. Paul Ramsey has argued that a parent cannot consent to a non-therapeutic experiment for his child:

> To attempt to consent for a child to be made an experimental subject is to treat a child as not a child. It is to treat him as if he were an adult person who has consented to become a joint adventurer in the common cause of medical research . . . No child or adult incompetent can choose to become a participating member of medical undertakings, and no one else on earth should decide to subject these people to investigations having no relation to their own treatment. That is a canon of loyalty to them. This they claim of us by being a human child or incompetent.[1]

Our question is not the same as the question of volunteering a child for a non-therapeutic experiment, but Ramsey's point should nevertheless be kept in mind. Children make certain demands of us simply because they are children. We cannot decide for them as we think they might decide for themselves if they were adults. A child is not an adult. Parents should be very reluctant to choose anything for a child that we would not let an adult do unless he truly consented.

There is another dimension of the parent-child relationship that might be commented on. That is the emotion in the decision-making. One sometimes hears of parents who decide not to have their child treated and who then change their minds after they get to know the child better. Would it have been better for the parents to keep more of a distance, to keep from becoming emotionally involved? Does a close involvement with the child tend to cloud the issues or put things in better perspective? When we keep in mind that we are talking about a parent-child relationship, there is no clear reason to think that emotion should be avoided. In fact, there is something very basic missing if the parents do not feel some attachment toward the child. Such attachment should be very much a part of the atmosphere in which the decision is made.

There is a real possibility, of course, that the parents' initial emotional response to the birth of a deformed child will be one of rejection or even of repulsion rather than one of attachment. A birth of that sort is usually such a shock, and our expectations of a normal baby so high, that some very definite negative attitudes toward the child are common. These negative emotional responses should not be feared, but they should not be permitted to play a very important part in the decision-making. They are likely to be temporary and do not have the same place in the normal parent-child relationship as the positive emotional responses. We do not need to worry about the parents' tender response to the child as being detrimental to a good moral decision, but we do need to be concerned about the rejection attitude. The tender response should be part of the parent-child relationship; the rejection response, though normal and expectable, should not be part of the on-going relationship.

That parents should accept moral responsibility for their severely handicapped child means more than that they are the ones who must make the decision. Moral responsibility means accepting the consequences of that decision. It means taking upon themselves, if necessary, the difficult tasks that result from the decision. It means continued parental care for the child regardless of the decision. Moral responsibility does not seem to be fully assumed by parents who let the hospital staff watch a baby die slowly while constantly absenting themselves. Nor are parents acting responsibly who have life-saving treatment for their abnormal child but later do very little to help that child have as rich a life as possible.

To what extent must the decision be their own for parents to be acting in a morally responsible manner? Are parents acting responsibly if, for example, they decide the question of treatment for their child by doing whatever their moral counselor suggests? Such a decision might be morally responsible. Parents may do whatever the counselor suggests because they greatly admire the thinking and the moral sensitivities of the person who gives the advice and because they themselves are having a hard time reaching a decision. There is nothing irresponsible about that *provided* they made the advisor's position their own. They have made that decision their own if they blame no one else if there are regrets later on; they are acting responsibly if they can explain to their own satisfaction the reasons why it is better to take someone else's advice than to continue to wrestle with the decision themselves. Even if the parents do not fully understand the reasons given by the adviser for following a particular course of action, it can make good moral sense to do what he says because of the great confidence they have in that person or in the tradition or church that he represents. Moral responsibility does not mean that everyone must always decide every question for himself; it can be very wise at times to follow the teaching of someone who, they feel, knows better than they what should be done. What has to be avoided is the Adolf Eichmann syndrome, the feeling that one is not responsible because he is only acting according to the commands or suggestions of someone else.

The parents of a severely handicapped child have a very heavy responsibility. They should do whatever they can to let others help them bear that burden well and make sound decisions.

# 6
# The Role of the Public

There are two fundamental questions to be asked in this final chapter, as we try to determine the responsibility of the general public in the care and protection of handicapped infants. In what ways, if any, should the law be used to restrict parents from doing whatever they determine best in the care of their child? What obligations do citizens have to provide, through the state, care and education for handicapped children? It is in responding to these two questions that we can consider the role of society in ensuring that the most important values are protected.

The first question involves, in a sense, the role of the public in the decision-making. We have considered the role of the parents, the medical staff, and the moral counselor. We need now to consider the role of the rest of us. All of us need to decide whether we think the state should intervene by setting limits and, if so, what those limits should be. The law is the tool that we, usually through our representatives, use to express our public involvement in an issue. The first question, then, is the question of how we want to see parental authority regulated or restricted by law.

While the first question involves the negative side of public involvement, that of setting limits to prohibit unnecessary evil or harm, the second question has to do with the positive side, that of providing care and opportunities for others. What should we recognize as obligations in this area and what do we want to see the state do in the name of all of us?

We are constantly using the law to regulate matters that we, the public, consider important. We have laws prohibiting killing because life is considered one of our most basic goods.

We have laws prohibiting theft because property is important to us. We have laws against excessive pollution because the quality of our environment is seen as important. We have laws requiring children to attend school because we consider education important. We use the law to protect those values that we, as a society, consider important; the law is, in a sense, the expression of our public values.

The contemporary emphasis on individual freedom is posing something of a challenge to the practice of using the law to express the values of society (or of many within society). Or, to put it differently, the value of freedom is beginning to have an impact on the legal situation. There is a movement to abolish laws that prohibit actions which are "victimless." There is a great deal of emphasis on the right to privacy. The desire to have the laws of our society protect freedom and privacy as much as possible may simply be another way of wanting the legal situation to reflect our values, but there is something of a difference. The emphasis on freedom and privacy may mean refraining from prohibiting actions of individuals where emphasis on other values may mean prohibiting those actions.

Since there are different moral positions being taken on the question of how to care for severely handicapped infants, the question of the best laws to regulate the situation becomes very difficult. Should we attempt to use the law to protect those values that we, in our moral thinking, have concluded are very important? Even if many others, possibly parents personally involved, disagree with us? Or is it possible to separate our moral views from the laws we write? Before we can get to specific suggestions about the best laws in regard to the handicapped infant issue, it is necessary to consider the whole question of the relationship between moral values and the law.

## Morality and the Law

Living as we do in a morally pluralistic society, one of the most difficult questions that we are faced with is the question of what sort of legal policy to support on issues that most people see as debatable moral questions. It is easy to find ourselves pulled in two different directions. On the one hand, we do not want to prohibit individuals from acting according to their own moral views if that can be avoided; after all, there is always the possibility that we ourselves may find the law prohibiting something that we see as demanded by morality. On the other hand, we recognize that laws are often necessary to protect individuals from harm and that it is impossible to live together with any peace and harmony at all unless some are forced to do what they do not want to do. It is often difficult to know when to place the emphasis on respecting individual moral opinion and individual freedom and when to place the emphasis on enforcing certain behavior in order to protect persons and values.

We might consider carefully three ways which are sometimes proposed as resolutions of this dilemma. Some argue that since we are living in a morally pluralistic society, the more permissive law is usually the better law. We should not attempt to impose our moral views on others. Some suggest that the values and moral views of the majority should be reflected in laws. It is impossible to avoid imposing the views of some on others, but if we always make sure that it is the majority's views being reflected in the law we will be doing as little imposing as possible. Others insist that the individual should have laws passed which reflect his own moral views. After all, once you have determined what is the right thing to do in a particular situation, it only makes sense to try to get others to act that way as well. We will look at each of these suggestions in turn.

There is something to be said in support of the argument that we should try to avoid imposing our moral views on those who disagree. The individual should be as free as possible to live his own life according to his best moral insights. Privacy and the freedom of conscience are fundamental conditions for the good life and they should be protected as much as possible. The law should be looked upon as a practical tool for regulating human interaction and not primarily as a tool for enforcing moral conformity.

This does not, however, immediately lead us to the conclusion that the more permissive law is usually the better one. The fact that some, in our morally pluralistic society, do not agree that all races are equal is no reason to remove anti-slavery laws or anti-discrimination laws. The fact that some, perhaps many, do not think that it is wrong to cheat on income tax returns does not mean that we should have no laws prohibiting that type of behavior. It is very difficult to think of any law which does not impose the values of some on others who have different values. Perhaps the question that the individual should ask himself when trying to decide whether a certain law is a good one is not whether he would be imposing his moral position on someone else, but whether the law would do more good than harm. The denial of freedom of conscience to certain people may be part of the harm done, but it is not all that has to be considered. The good that is done in protecting persons and in supporting standards and values in the long run may outweigh the harm involved in imposing certain behavior on those who are not morally convinced of that behavior.

The abortion discussion and the Supreme Court's decision on abortion have given some evidence of what happens when the focus is on the freedom of the individual to act according to his own morality. Without making any specific criticisms of the Supreme Court's decision and without suggesting what type of abortion laws we should have, a couple observations can be made on the permissive law approach by keeping the abortion question in mind.

The desire to highlight individual freedom usually seems to involve seeing things in an individualistic way. Even when the provision is included that actions may be prohibited if "someone else will be hurt," the tendency may be to quickly assume that no one else will be hurt. It seems pretty clear that for many the conviction that the fetus is not a separate "someone" followed from, did not precede, the conviction that a woman should be free to do what she thinks is morally right in regard to abortion. The emphasis on individual freedom means an emphasis on the individual. And an emphasis on the individual usually involves seeing persons as separate, not intimately affected by the activities of one another. There is a tendency to be very quick to conclude that others will not be hurt, that others are not involved, that it is something affecting only the individual's own life. This, then, is one reason to hesitate about approaching the legal side of difficult moral questions primarily in terms of not restricting individual moral freedom—it is too easy to get things out of proper focus and to see only one side of the picture.

It is not hard to find examples where the question of abortion and the law is seen primarily as a question of religious freedom and not primarily in terms of abortion itself. James Nelson has this to say about the Supreme Court's ruling and his reasons for supporting it:

> What is at stake is not the rights of anti-abortion groups to espouse their theological and moral convictions, educate their members, and seek to influence others. These rights are constitutionally guaranteed . . . Rather, what is at stake is the freedom of sizeable numbers of citizens *from* the religious views of others with whom they sincerely disagree. Surely there are moral issues on which a broad consensus does exist, convictions which for many persons are based upon religious beliefs, and for which the power of civil law is appropriate. Racial segregation is a case in point. The case of abortion differs, however. Here the moral position is tied much more directly with the theological convictions of *particular* groups. Here a broad public consensus is lacking. In matters of abortion choice in the early months of pregnancy, what many consider a sin ought not to be made a crime, and the court was right in insisting upon the religious neutrality of the state at this point.[1]

The freedom of conscience of the individual is one important dimension when considering abortion laws, but it is not, it must be insisted, the only thing or even the most important thing that is at stake. Nelson and others who speak this way do something of a disservice by painting the whole picture as one of moral or religious freedom. We cannot see all the social implications of an abortion law by looking at only one dimension. There are other values involved, particularly the value of human fetal life. There is something to be said for allowing as much freedom as possible when no consensus can be reached, but I am not so sure that that should be the case when it is, possibly, human life that is being destroyed. There may be a danger of becoming overly concerned about denying freedom and not sufficiently concerned about protecting other values.

The desire not to impose a position by restricting behavior may in itself be imposing a position on those who do not agree. Almost any law restricts some from acting according to their convictions, even a ruling which *permits* something. The Supreme Court ruling prohibited states from outlawing abortion during the first two trimesters. What that means is that those who are convinced that abortion is the unjustified killing of innocent human persons are prohibited from doing some of the things they think they should do as a result of those convictions. They are prohibited from using state law to protect these new lives. In some cases, this is imposing a moral position on those who do not agree; it is not permitting them to act in full accord with their convictions. Obviously, this is not an imposition in quite the same sense as it would be in the case of a woman being denied an abortion who is morally convinced that it is the right thing to do. But to approach these questions from the starting point of trying to avoid imposing values on others may very well lead to failure to recognize that all laws impose restrictions on freedom.

To insist that restrictive laws be abolished whenever a question is morally disputed is to take one particular moral value, that of individual freedom, and to attempt to have a legal policy that supports that moral value. That is not very different from others attempting to have the law reflect their moral values. Perhaps the question is not whether moral values should be imposed or supported by law, but *which* values should be imposed or supported by law. In the quote above, Nelson suggested that the Court was acting in a religiously neutral way by its decision. Its decision did, though, clearly support one value, that of privacy, over others.

We should not be too quick to assume, then, that since we are living in a morally pluralistic society it is usually better to have very permissive laws. It is true that we do not want to impose restrictions upon another's moral freedom unnecessarily. But it is also true that we should not be so concerned for freedom of conscience that we lose sight of other important considerations.

It is sometimes said that we should try to adopt those laws which reflect the values of the majority. After all, we live in a democratic society where the will of the majority often does, in fact, become law. We should accept that fact and support only those laws that do reflect the moral values of the majority. We can maintain our divergent moral positions, of course, and try to persuade others, try to gain a majority for our position, but our legal policy should be to support only that which has the backing of the majority. Nothing else is as fully aware of our type of democracy.

This argument does recognize that the principle of majority rule is a very important safeguard against tyranny. Freedom and democracy should not be equated with rule by the majority (the majority can support very undemocratic measures), but rule by the majority serves as a very useful means of trying to protect freedom. What an individual believes in should not become the law for others unless a majority of the lawmakers are persuaded that it is appropriate.

It is one thing to say that something should not become law unless the majority (of the legislators) think that it is for the good of the people. It is an entirely different thing to say that we should not propose or support a law which does not initially have the support of the majority. That would permit very little opportunity for persuasion. If an individual thinks that a particular practice is wrong and so detrimental to the values of society that it ought to be outlawed, one of the best ways of trying to persuade others of his understanding is to advocate legislation, even though he is very aware that the majority do not agree with him, at least yet. If he and those who agree with him can get the majority to accept the bill, then there is no longer a question of imposing their position on the majority. But if a minority position should never even be proposed as a possible law, there would be much less opportunity for development in our thinking on what constitutes a good law.

It should be recognized, as well, that the majority may not

always be acting for the good; there is always a danger that the majority may be supporting practices that are very harmful to some. The fact that a law is the will of the majority in no way guarantees that it is just or even that it is democratic in the sense of truly respecting freedom. Whether one supports a particular law or not should not be based on whether the proposed law has the support of the majority, but whether he thinks such a law is likely to be of benefit to the members of society. His primary concern should be the consequences of such a law. It is necessary that the will of the majority determine the fate of a proposed law in the end, but there is no reason to presume that a bill which is initially unpopular would necessarily be bad legislation. The majority can be mistaken and the individual should not hesitate to try to persuade others to his point of view, even when his view represents an unpopular position.

The third suggestion that should be commented on is that the individual try to have those laws passed which reflect his own moral views. Clearly there is some validity in this approach. Particularly if the individual's moral views are based upon a concern for consequences, his legal thinking should not be drastically different from his moral thinking. Legal policy, too, needs to be based upon concern for consequences, how behavior should be regulated so that the most good results. If one is convinced that a certain practice is immoral because it is destructive of some very important value in society, then it would not seem to be out of place to seek a law to restrict that practice.

But questions of morality and questions of legality are not exactly the same. Morality has to do with what we think should be done, how we and others should act in order to respect those values that we hold to be most important. Legality has to do with the type of behavior that should be required of people. Moral issues and legal issues both focus on what is for the good of individuals and the good of society, but the implications may be somewhat different. When we advocate a certain type of behavior as being the best morally, we need to assume some responsibility for the consequences of that type of behavior. When we are successful in getting a particular type of behavior prohibited by law, we must recognize not only some responsibility for the consequences of the way people act as a result of the law but also some responsibility for the difficulties resulting from the enforcement of that law. A law cannot be enforced without some cost. We might very well want to argue, for example, that adultery is immoral because it is a betrayal of the trust and loyalty that needs to exist between spouses if we are going to have the sort of family life that our society needs. But it is something else to say that adultery should be prohibited by a law that would be vigorously enforced. In the first place, there is no good reason to think that such a law would significantly strengthen the trust and loyalty of spouses. Secondly, the consequences of the enforcement of such a law might be quite undesirable, such things, perhaps, as widespread invasion of privacy and a heavy burden on an already overburdened judicial system. One might very well conclude that such a law might do more harm than good. The stand one takes morally in this case may not be what he would like to see enforced by law.

The law is a tool to be used to try to achieve the most desirable, or least undesirable, consequences for society. Sometimes that means we should not attempt to make illegal what we consider immoral. Sometimes that might mean we should attempt to do just that. We need to remember that the consequences that may be affected by the law include the standards or values that we as a culture adopt publicly and teach the young. We may wish that it were not so, but certainly some persons tend to think that something which is legal is also moral. Their values are largely shaped by our laws and customs. It would not be confusing the relationship between moral issues and legal ones to propose a law or oppose a law partly on the basis of the impact that it is likely to have on our cultural values and moral standards. That is an important consequence.

One's legal stand should not, then, be exactly the same as one's moral position in all cases, but neither should one forget moral concerns in taking a legal stand. Not everything that one considers immoral should be outlawed, but neither should one hesitate to act legally on his moral convictions of what would be best for society. A good law is one that produces results benefi-

cial to society. The judgment about whether results are beneficial or not always remains a value judgment. Just as it would be
a mistake to attempt to have the law reproduce all one's views
on private morality, so it would be a mistake to pretend that
decisions about laws can be totally "practical" without moral
values being involved.

On the basis of the foregoing reflections, we can make
these recommendations on how to approach the legal side of
disputed moral questions. Act with an awareness of the danger
of restricting the moral freedom of those who disagree, but do
not allow this concern for individual freedom to eclipse other
concerns. Recognize that the rule of the majority is an important safeguard against tyranny, but do not hesitate to support a
proposed law simply because it does not initially reflect the values of the majority. Do not apologize if a legal proposal is
based upon personal moral convictions regarding what is good
for society, but remember that it is not the same thing to say
that something is illegal as it is to say that it is immoral. These
recommendations are kept in mind as we suggest legal policy
regarding the treatment of severely handicapped infants.

## The Law and the Handicapped Infant

Our goals here are somewhat limited. We do not propose
to analyze current laws which may affect the type of treatment
given to severely handicapped infants. Nor are we suggesting
what new laws may have to be written. What we do hope to
provide is a description of what the laws should accomplish. We
will let others decide whether the present laws succeed in protecting what needs to be protected or exactly how they should
be rewritten if they do not. Here we will simply suggest what a
study of the problem shows to be the public's obligation to protect the child.

The first point that needs to be made is that we should not
permit *direct* killing of an infant, no matter how severely deformed and no matter how inevitable his death. It is understandable that some would seek to end the child's suffering

quickly and painlessly when there is no hope for survival or when the decision has been made not to treat. Though it is understandable, society should not permit it. We simply cannot permit someone, even a parent, to kill a helpless child. We need to protect and defend the helpless against those who wish to do them physical harm, even when that killing results from a desire to be merciful and loving. The role of parents does not extend to the authority to kill; the rest of us have an obligation to step in to protect the child against such an act.

The mercy killing of a deformed or handicapped child is not the same as the calculated killing of someone else in the pursuit of personal gain. Mercy killing of this sort is certainly not the same as first degree murder and that needs to be recognized by law. But we do need to prohibit such killing and to make the punishment serious enough to emphasize that we cannot permit individuals to kill other individuals, no matter what the motive. Human life is one of those fundamental values that society should protect by law, all the more so when it is the life of a helpless infant who is incapable of protecting himself or of making his will known.

We are speaking here, it might be repeated, of direct killing, those actions which directly cause the death of the child, such as a lethal injection or suffocation. Actions which make the death probable or even inevitable but which do not in themselves cause the death, such as turning off mechanical support systems or refusing permission for an operation, should not be considered direct killing. It is probably necessary for the law to make a sharp distinction between direct killing and letting die. Direct killing cannot be permitted if we are going to insist upon the right to life of everyone. Letting die should be legal or not depending upon the circumstances, as will be discussed below.

This absolute legal prohibition of direct killing of deformed infants may seem questionable and perhaps hypocritical to some. The law of the land permits abortion and much effort is being expended to diagnose prenatally so that abnormal fetuses can be destroyed. It is legal to kill at one point in time and it is frequently done when an abnormality is suspected. Why should it be illegal to kill some weeks later when an unsuspected ab-

normality is revealed by birth? The fact that abortion is legal
does not mean that one must, to be consistent, permit mercy
killing of infants as well. (We will not pursue here the question
of whether the present abortion law is a good one.) The law is
not hypocritical when it draws lines. The line should be drawn
at that point at which the public is convinced it is necessary to
restrict behavior. Even if abortion is legal until late in the pregnancy, there is no reason to therefore permit killing of abnormal babies. There can be no doubt that a live child, after birth,
is a fellow human being. As such, he deserves protection against
destruction regardless of what our legal policy on abortion is.

Others may ask why such a big distinction should be made
in the law between killing and letting die. Isn't there something
wrong about making more of being responsible for death in one
way than of being responsible in another way? For the law to
distinguish between killing and letting die does not mean that all
cases of letting a child die are to be legal while all cases of
killing are not. It is, rather, the simple recognition that two
types of behavior are somewhat different and, as a result,
should be distinguished so that they can be dealt with more adequately.

In addition to prohibiting direct killing, the law needs to
protect children from their parents in other ways as well. Most
parents can, of course, be counted upon to act for the welfare of
their children, but there are enough instances of child abuse and
child neglect to make it perfectly clear that the public cannot
presume that all parents will always act in ways that are beneficial to their children. Nor should we think that parents who en-
danger the welfare of their children are always acting out of
hostility. They may very well be doing what they think is best
for the child. The public's obligation is to enter into the parent-
child relationship if necessary to protect the child not only from
the hostile parent but also from the well-meaning, but harmful,
parent. Because it is not always easy to know what constitutes
harm for the child and because it is important that parents have
the primary place in the raising of their children, the law's intervention to protect the child must be minimal, undertaken only

when there is clear evidence of very serious danger to the welfare of the child.

In the case of severely handicapped infants, the law should permit parents to decide whether or not life-saving treatment should be undertaken or prolonged except in those cases where there is little reason to withhold treatment. The decision to let a child die rather than have him treated should not immediately be presumed to be one of neglect. The law should not impose treatment at all cost, but only prohibit the decision to let die when the child's condition does not warrant that decision.

The law should clearly prohibit letting a child die in cases where it does not take medical intervention to save the life of the child. Parents should not be permitted, for example, to starve a child to death because they decided that his condition makes his life not worth living. The public has the obligation to insist that parents provide their children with minimum care, such as adequate food and shelter.

When it takes medical intervention to stop a child from dying, the case is somewhat different. There we should recognize the parents' responsibility to decide what treatment, if any, is appropriate. But even here, they should be permitted to decide for themselves only within certain limits. The public has an obligation to insist that, under certain conditions, treatment must be undertaken whether parents want it or not. Court orders that blood transfusions be given to children even when their parents object to such procedures on religious grounds are examples of legal intervention to save the life of a child by overriding the wishes of parents who are conscientiously following their own moral convictions. We can rightfully use the law to counteract parents' wishes and save a child when such ordinary measures can save that life. A child is entitled to that kind of life-saving care, even when the parents think it best not to provide it. The public, by enforcing such treatment, is not denying that parents have the primary role of caring for their children. It is only recognizing that there are limits to the authority that parents have over the lives of their children.

The law should not attempt to spell out precisely which

conditions warrant the decision to let a child die. That would be too restrictive of an intervention in medicine and in family decisions, even if it were feasible. The law should simply make it possible for the state to intervene where the right of the child to normal medical treatment is being denied. The concept of normal or ordinary care may be the best one that can be used in law. It would allow the parents to make their own decision, but would set some limits to their authority to let a child of theirs die untreated. The notion of normal or ordinary would allow those directly involved to set the standards of what should be permitted, which is the way it should be. The concept would also permit development as time goes on, as what is ordinarily done changes; that, too, is as it should be. Such a law would not be perfect, of course. It may impose treatment where it is not really called for, simply because most parents do decide to treat in those cases. Or it may permit a child to be deprived of an opportunity to live without sufficient reason if a relatively large number of other persons do the same thing. But, at least at the present, it would seem that the law must permit these possible abuses. The public cannot allow parents to decide to do just anything they want with their children. On the other hand, it must allow those most intimately involved, parents and physicians, to set the basic standards of what is proper care.

Making it clear that the state has the right to enforce normal or ordinary care of an infant may not protect against parental neglect in the care of their children in all cases, but it can protect against the most serious denials of the deformed child's right to life. And, if we want to maintain parental authority over their children, protection against the most serious abuses is all that we can feasibly accomplish by law.

We suggest, then, that the law be used to protect the lives of handicapped children in three ways:

1. Direct killing should not be permitted.
2. Letting a child die when medical treatment is not needed should not be permitted.
3. Letting a child die by withholding treatment should be

permitted only if it is a normal or ordinary way of responding to this type of condition.

## Other Obligations

It is most important that the public recognize that its role is not just a negative role, that of protecting the lives of infants. It also has the obligation to help parents provide care and education for handicapped infants. This is the other side of the obligation to insist that parents are not always free to let their handicapped children die. Concern for the quality of life means that we do not disregard the value of life itself by being too quick to let a handicapped infant die; it must also mean that we are concerned about the type of life lived by those handicapped children who survive. A handicapped child imposes a very heavy burden on a family. It is the obligation of the public to share that burden to some extent.

We have, of course, long recognized some such obligation. States have provided institutions of total care as well as educational facilities for the handicapped. Yet sometimes we seem to have a certain reluctance to invest too much talent and energy and money in these efforts. Obviously our resources are limited and we cannot always do everything that we would like to see done. But we should be sure that it is the fact of our limited resources that is responsible for less than ideal care for the handicapped, not our limited sense of responsibility.

In various parts of this book, we have emphasized the importance of caring for the weak and the helpless and the underprivileged who are in our midst. A sign of a culture's moral strength is the way people love and care for those who are not able to care for themselves. Admiring, as we naturally do, physical health and strength and mental ability, it is always tempting to try to ignore those who are physically or mentally handicapped. They disturb our world somewhat and we may want to pretend that they do not exist. But these temptations can be overcome.

The way in which the public accepts its obligation to help the parents to care for the handicapped can take a variety of forms. We will comment only on the most obvious here.

All of us need to help to bear one another's burdens. And this might include financial burdens. Having a severely handicapped child, who needs much special care, both medical and other, can be a great expense to the family. Society should recognize the importance of helping share that expense, at least in catastrophic cases. Medical expenses in particular can be very great. There may very well be some serious disadvantages to a form of national health insurance, where all taxpayers help to pay for the medical expenses of those who need care; but some such way of recognizing the obligation of the public to help finance the medical care of those who need very expensive care seems demanded. One of the ideas behind any form of insurance is that no one person or family will be hit too hard if many share the expense. It is a good idea and probably should be expanded further in medical care. The rest of us should recognize an obligation to keep those who are ill through no fault of their own from being completely overwhelmed by medical expenses.

There are times when children are so severely deformed or handicapped that the families simply cannot care for them at home. This burden, too, the public should be willing to assume. State-run homes and institutions for the handicapped sometimes have a reputation for low quality care and for a hopeless atmosphere. We should recognize, though, that these institutions do provide a very important service; they pick up a burden the parents can no longer carry. They are a recognition of the public obligation to help share the care of these unfortunate children. But just as we should not feel that enough has been done when we prohibit parents from arbitrarily letting their children die, so we should not think that enough has been done when state-supported homes have been provided to care for the severely handicapped or the severely retarded. We must also do whatever we can to see that the children in these homes are treated with dignity and respect.

Another way in which all of us need to recognize an obligation to help provide care for handicapped children is in the area of education or training. We have long ago decided that education of children is such an important value or right that it should be provided whether individuals can afford it or not. It has often been recognized, as well, that retarded and other handicapped children need special education and that this too should be provided at public expense. Once again, though, the public obligation is not just to see that educational opportunities are provided, but to see that the quality of this education is good. These children probably need education and training opportunities more than a normal child does if they are going to have as rich a life as possible. So we should not hesitate to invest more, relatively speaking, of our educational efforts and dollars in this kind of special education. The public's role in regard to these disadvantaged is not just to see that the necessities for sustaining life are provided, but also to make sure that there are real opportunities for developing potential and talents.

There are other ways as well in which society should recognize a need to help some of the least fortunate among us. It will not be too difficult to recognize ways in which the public can contribute to the care of the handicapped as long as we see these children as individuals to be loved and helped. The most basic obligation that the public has is always to recognize that any child, no matter how severely handicapped or deformed, is a very important human person.

*Chapter 1*

1. See "In Brief," *The Hastings Center Report,* 4 (September, 1974), 16.
2. "What Would You Do If the Problem Were Yours?" *Medical World News,* 13 (July 14, 1972), 40.
3. "On the Birth of a Severely Handicapped Infant," *The Hastings Center Report,* 3 (September, 1973), 10.
4. Bernard Bard, "The Right to Die," *The Atlantic Monthly,* 221 (April, 1968), 60-62.
5. "The Courts and the Severely Defective Child," *The Detroit Free Press* (March 10, 1974), p. 6-D.
6. Raymond S. Duff and A. G. M. Campbell, "Moral and Ethical Dilemmas in the Special-Care Nursery," *The New England Journal of Medicine,* 289 (October 25, 1973), 891-893.
7. James Nelson, *Human Medicine* (Minneapolis, 1973), p. 98.
8. *Ibid.,* p. 99.
9. Frederick Osborn, quoted by Paul Ramsey, *Fabricated Man* (New Haven, 1970), p. 4.
10. Nelson, *op. cit.,* p. 98.
11. See the discussion of the clinical definition of death in Paul Ramsey, *The Patient as Person* (New Haven, 1970), pp. 59-112.
12. Robert Rizzo and Joseph Yonder, "Definition and Criteria of Death," *The Linacre Quarterly,* 40 (November, 1973), 228.
13. *Ibid.,* p. 230.
14. Joseph Fletcher, "The Right To Die: A Theologian Comments," *The Atlantic Monthly,* 221 (April, 1968), 63-64.
15. See especially Elizabeth Kubler-Ross, *On Death and Dying* (New York, 1969).

*Chapter 2*

1. Charles McFadden, *Medical Ethics* (Philadelphia, 1967), p. 122.
2. Daniel Callahan, *Abortion: Law, Choice and Morality* (New York, 1970), Chapter 11.
3. Tabitha Powledge and Sharmon Sollitto, "Prenatal Diagnosis —The Past and the Future," *The Hastings Center Report,* 4 (November, 1974), 11-14.

4. Quoted by Karen Lebacqz, "Prenatal Diagnosis and Selective Abortion," *The Linacre Quarterly*, 40 (May, 1973), 116.

5. Gerald Kelly, *Medico-Moral Problems* (St. Louis, 1958), p. 129.

6. Daniel Callahan, "The Quality of Life: What Does It Mean?" in George Devine (ed.) *That They May Live* (New York, 1972), pp. 12-13.

7. Joseph Fletcher, "The Right to Die: A Theologian Comments," *The Atlantic Monthly*, 221 (April, 1968), 62.

8. Leonard J. Weber, "Human Death as Neocortical Death: The Ethical Context," *The Linacre Quarterly*, 41 (May, 1974), 106-113.

## Chapter 3

1. See Paul and Anne Ehrlich, *The End of Affluence* (New York, 1974).

2. David H. Smith, "On Letting Some Babies Die," *The Hastings Center Studies*, 2 (May, 1974), 37-46.

3. *Ibid.*, p. 45.

4. *Ibid.*, p. 42.

5. *Ibid.*, p. 44.

6. *Ibid.*, p. 46.

7. Joseph Fletcher, "The Right to Die: A Theologian Comments," *The Atlantic Monthly*, 221 (April, 1968), 62.

8. *Ibid.*, p. 63.

9. *Ibid.*, p. 64.

10. *Ibid.*

11. *Ibid.*

12. *Ibid.*

13. *Ibid.*, p. 63.

14. *Ibid.*

15. Warren T. Reich, "On the Birth of a Severely Handicapped Infant," *The Hastings Center Report*, 3 (September, 1973), 11.

16. *Ibid.*

17. Warren T. Reich, "Testimony Before the Subcommittee on Health of the Committee on Labor and Public Welfare, U. S. Senate," unpublished (June 11, 1974), p. 2.

18. *Ibid.*, p. 6.

19. *Ibid.*, p. 5.

20. *Ibid.*, pp. 1-2.

21. Reich, "On the Birth of a Severely Handicapped Infant," *loc. cit.*, p. 11.

22. *Ibid.*

23. *Ibid.*

24. Richard A. McCormick, "To Save or Let Die: The Dilemma of Modern Medicine," *The Journal of the American Medical Association*, 229 (July 8, 1974), 175.

25. *Ibid.*, p. 174.

26. *Ibid.*, p. 175.

27. *Ibid.*

28. *Ibid.*

29. *Ibid.*, p. 176.

30. *Ibid.*

*Chapter 4*

1. Joseph Fletcher, "Indicators of Humanhood: A Tentative Profile of Man," *The Hastings Center Report*, 2 (November, 1972), 1.

2. Karen Lebacqz, "Prenatal Diagnosis and Selective Abortion," *The Linacre Quarterly*, 40 (May, 1973), 126.

3. Warren T. Reich, "On the Birth of a Severely Handicapped Infant," *The Hastings Center Report*, 3 (September, 1973), 11.

4. Richard A. McCormick, "Notes on Moral Theology: April-September, 1974," *Theological Studies*, 36 (March, 1975), 122.

5. Gerald Kelly, *Medico-Moral Problems* (St. Louis, 1958), p. 129.

6. Richard A. McCormick, "To Save or Let Die: The Dilemma of Modern Medicine," *The Journal of the American Medical Association*, 229 (July 8, 1974), 176.

*Chapter 5*

1. Paul Ramsey, *The Patient as Person* (New Haven, 1970), p. 14.

*Chapter 6*

1. James Nelson, *Human Medicine* (Minneapolis, 1973), pp. 56-57.